MYSELF

Van Fisher

MYSELF

THE AUTOBIOGRAPHY OF
JOHN R. COMMONS

THE UNIVERSITY OF WISCONSIN PRESS

MADISON, 1964

Published 1963 by
The University of Wisconsin Press
430 Sterling Court
Madison 6, Wisconsin

Paperback edition, 1964

Formerly published (1934)
by the Macmillan Company
Printed in
the United States of America
Library of Congress
Catalog Card Number 63-15619

CONTENTS

ILLUSTRATIONS

MYSELF

MYSELF

I

TO MY "FRIDAY NITERS"

I WRITE this biography in sorrow and doubt. It would not be done except for the insistence of my Friday Niters. Several generations of them, on my seventieth anniversary, 1932, presented me with a fund of $1,500 for travel and recovery of health. They set up a Labor Research Library in the University under my name and portrait. There are deposited all the books written by my students, along with my own books and articles covering forty years, in uniform red binding.

Here I am, beyond the biblical years, almost out of action since 1930, quite despondent that my working hours are forced down to two, or three, or nothing, with prolonged vacations and one two-hour lecture per week, living on a Carnegie pension and an emeritus salary. I cannot understand these benefactions from my past and present students, at a time when they cannot afford it and when I look into myself and see many years of mistakes and misdemeanors. Even the so-called "courage," which they played up in a leaflet commemorating my seventieth anniversary, I know was really timidity. I was always experimenting and always trying out theories on other people.

There was no reason or logic in it—a child's curiosity that always got me into trouble or inconsistency.

I have tried to analyze the friendship of my Friday Niters. I trace it back thirty years to the time when I came to Wisconsin and had given up my first ideas of teaching. I began simply to tell my classes personal stories of my mistakes, doubts and explorations, just as they happened to occur to me, injecting my generalizations, comparisons and all kinds of social philosophies. This is the only way I can account for it. It is ignorance, not intellect, that makes humanity kin. I often answer their questions, "I don't know." I think my students were more interested in my telling these stories and my dubious interpretations than they were when I attempted to expound systematically the consistent theories of economics. I was always casting doubt on the latter and getting my students mixed up. One of them, just returned from a brave career as a nurse at Amiens, told the Friday Niters that in the first year she thought she was getting the last word in economics, but that in the second year I contradicted everything I said the first year.

This inconsistency, I am afraid, is what they want in my autobiography. Somehow they probably thought that if, during fifty years, I could work my way out by inconsistencies, then there was hope for them. Perhaps too, they liked it that I did not take myself seriously. How could I take myself seriously when I was "putting over" something grand but contradictory to what I previously or afterwards put over. I could do this without realizing my inconsistency because my principal endowment is what Mark Twain called his "forgetter."

But now I take myself seriously. I cannot work. I feel myself a failure in my own home. Why should I parade? Here I sit with only one child left out of six. My oldest served in the War, with honors for bravery from the English and Russian governments, but disappeared from my home in 1930, under a persecution mania. Four died in infancy. My wife, who for thirty years saved me from blunders or got me out of them, and who read and corrected all my manuscripts, has been gone six years. My sickliness from childhood has often knocked me out of my work and sent me wandering over the earth looking for something new. These culminated in this collapse, which began in 1930, and now I cannot travel any more but must sit at my window reading detective stories and looking out on beautiful Lake Mendota and distant hills, which, in their continuous change every hour of the day, are my substitute for travel. Then, too, I have saved no money, and in these distressing times, with my relatives in need of help more serious than my own, I worry about that mortgage which apparently is greater than my home will sell for.

Yet the intent listening and the generous gifts of my Friday Niters have made me egotistic. I begin to compare myself with the great scientists of the past. Newton worked intensely for twenty-five years and then went insane. Darwin and Spencer could work only two or three hours a day at an age when I was working eight to twelve hours, seven days a week. A genius can do in a few years, if he works intensely, more than I could do in fifty years by intensive study. The genius can see through to the bottom of things without digging, but I must dig and re-dig.

And so I could round up my publications after seventy years of age only because my students, latterly become colleagues, sometimes financed by the University or outside funds, had turned in to help me out. Life for me is no longer a physical existence. I do not care much for that. I only care to live long enough to get through the press my last two volumes covering fifty years of work.

Yet this is a beautiful world, after all, I must say. It is beautiful on account of friendship and collaboration. To me the beauty I get is the sight of my students, beginning as raw youth, gradually developing, out of their own energy and pertinacity, into leaders, scientists, authors, professors, doing important work, whether for labor, capitalists, governments, or succeeding generations of students. I live in them. In my own work and publications, for forty years, I have been collaborative with my students. I took them on trips and showed them how to interview. I found positions for them and insisted that they go out into the "cold world" before they graduated, and test their own and all economic theories by experience. They came back and corrected my errors. And though I have gained too much credit for what they got for me, yet I have at least been as scrupulous as possible in giving to them credit for what they have contributed. For I find that the noblest work in the world is not done for money—it is done for credit. And this pushing forward my students to the front, in so far as I had confidence in them suited to my knowledge of their experience and abilities, is perhaps one of the grounds for the friendship they reveal for me in my senility. Anyhow, there is where I get satisfaction and a kind of explanation of why they have worked for me without pay and have given me devoted assistance.

My Friday Niters are my graduate students and seniors —a group which has been meeting for the past thirty years. They bring in their friends, wives, and husbands. Formerly they met occasionally or individually, but for the past dozen years, at the suggestion of my wife, they have been meeting regularly, first at various restaurants, later at my home on Friday night, for a lap supper and two hours of talk. If they have done anything or are doing anything, other than studying, they are called upon to tell about it. Thus I get acquainted with them and keep up with the times. They introduce themselves to one another by reciting their own biographies. They become strong friends all round instead of breaking up in cliques. They help one another wherever they go. In distant cities they meet together as they did at my home. Each new generation keeps asking me to repeat what I did when I was a little boy and when I went out exploring.

I do not write this story as a chronology. It is the genesis of my ideas. My Friday Niters tell me, as I read it over to them, that now they begin to understand my lectures and theories. I jump back and forth over seventy years, thinking how my ideas began and where they ended. They end in my *Institutional Economics* and the third volume of *History of Labour in the United States*. Those volumes include much of my personal experience of the past forty years. What I there recite is omitted from this biography. In my *Institutional Economics* I give a full list of all my books and articles published since 1893, now filed by my Friday Niters in the John R. Commons Labor Research Library. It is quite an extensive list. Every title brings vividly to my mind the students and other persons I worked with and from whom I got my ideas. I now tell the story of how it came about.

II

NORTH AND SOUTH

MY mother was a Presbyterian, my father a Quaker. My mother's people came from Vermont by way of the Western Reserve, the territory owned by Connecticut in Colonial times but now the northeastern section of Ohio. They were farmers, but my mother landed as a school teacher, when she was twenty-eight years of age, at Richmond, Indiana, in 1854. My father's people, also farmers, came from North Carolina in 1812, escaping from the slavery country across the mountains and the Ohio River, and setting up the Western center of Quakerism at the same Richmond, Indiana. He was born in 1818. I was born, in 1862, at this meeting place of North and South. My earliest recollections were thrilling stories of their "underground railway," for the escape of Negroes to Canada, across my mother's Western Reserve and my father's Eastern Indiana. Liberty, equality, and defiance of the Fugitive Slave Law were my birthright, and Hoosierdom my education.

It required some years for my wife, Ella Downey, to weed out my Hoosierisms. Yet I often think how Indiana created an indigenous American school of letters unaffected by immigrants or the European classics imported by New England, and liberated from the repressions of

7

slavery in the South. I have often, in later years, wished that editors of magazines and books would let me talk Hoosier, which they would not.

As I look back upon my early years, I think there was something enticing in my father's Hoosier cronies at Winchester, Indiana. They sprawled back on their chairs, with their feet on the table, squirting tobacco juice and drawling their words lazily, but funny and keen. I have a picture of my father, writing editorials in this native attitude. I think that (until his old age, when he took a disastrous trip to Florida) he was never more than a hundred miles away from home—and then only across the state of Indiana. He and his cronies talked politics and science. Every one of them, in that Eastern section of Indiana, was a Republican, living on the battle cries of the Civil War, and everyone was a follower of Herbert Spencer, who was then the shining light of evolution and individualism. Several years later, in 1888, I was shocked, at a meeting of the American Economic Association, to hear Professor Ely denounce Herbert Spencer who had misled economists. I was brought up on Hoosierism, Republicanism, Presbyterianism, and Spencerism.

Here was a rift in my home. My mother was the strictest of Presbyterian Puritans. Both she and father brought me up on Fox's *Book of Martyrs,* for both Presbyterianism and Quakerism were versions of the English Puritanism of the Seventeenth Century. She was proud to trace her genealogy back to John Rogers who was burned at Smithfield by Bloody Mary, and she gave to me the name of that famous divine. She wanted me also to become a minister and induced the Presbyterian minister at

FATHER, 42, 1860

MOTHER, 34, 1860

SELF, CLARA, ALVIN, 1874

Union City to teach me Greek and Latin. She was graduated, in 1853, from Oberlin, on the Western Reserve,
which was the first coeducational institution in the country, and dated from 1833. Oberlin was also the first college to take Negroes. She financed my going to Oberlin,
in 1882, where I was graduated in 1888, thirty-five years
after her. She, too, was an ardent Republican, but active,
also, in the first "women's crusade" against the saloon. I
see now vividly the women around the "corner grocery"
in Union City, on their knees and praying, my mother
walking about as their leader.

She was set against evolution, Spencerism, Darwinism,
and my father's "hell-of-a-fellow" cronies, as they called
themselves. Yet I never heard a row or dispute between
them. Father just left the children to mother. He had
drifted away from the Quaker assembly, and was prepared
for Spencerism when it came along. I remember a Quaker
meeting at my home in Union City where they were praying for father. When I went to Richmond, thirty miles
away, I visited his Quaker parents and attended the Quaker
meetings. The Quakers never criticized my father to me,
neither did my mother. I think my home was a model of
liberty and toleration. Years afterwards I found the
philosophy of it in John Locke, whose writings were sur-
prisingly familiar to me, but were extended to the foundations of government and capitalism. I made John Locke
the subject of the first study in my *Institutional Economics*.

When I now look back on my mother's long years of
effort to maintain the strict orthodoxy of Calvinism in the
midst of this backsliding of her family and of all about
her, I see much the same persistency in my Communist

friends and students when nearly all the world is going Fascist, or Nazist, or Banker Capitalist. All their faith in a foreordained society of the proletariat is being shattered about them, yet they persist in the orthodoxy of Karl Marx. I feel sorry for them, as I did for mother. They are the Presbyterians of foreordained materialism. I give them a grade "A" nevertheless. I learned toleration in my home.

The Catholics also were included in our family acquaintance and toleration. Across the "alley" lived a family of Irish Catholic immigrants, almost the only representatives of that race and religion in Union City, which was my home on the state line of Ohio until I was sixteen years of age. The Catholic children were our playmates from my earliest recollections. I learned the Irish brogue as well as Hoosier. Neither father nor mother ever cautioned us against them. The Irish father was a drunkard, working at the railway roundhouse. The Irish mother supported him and their children, as well as her drunken brother. All of the children, except the eldest, grew up to be fine men and women, as I found years afterwards when I visited the mother at their original rackety, but now beautified, home. I found the father and uncle long since dead of tremens.

My mother, too, supported our family. In my earliest memory of her she was feeding two or three boarders and keeping roomers. This she was doing continuously, even at Oberlin until my graduation, where she was supporting, by means of a boarding house, her three children in the preparatory school and college. When she could work no longer I took her to Baltimore during the second year of my graduate study, where the two of us kept house together while I was at the University and she was taking the baths for her disabling rheumatism.

I had a biological advantage, at Oberlin, over my brother and sister, for I was the first-born and could go through to graduation before my mother's health gave out, but they had to stop in the freshman and junior years.

Years after mother's sacrifice for us, a lady professor at Oberlin said to me that, when she also was a student at Oberlin in the early 'fifties, all of them expected my mother to become one of the prominent women in the country. But she was now disappointed about my mother. I was startled and humiliated. I could only say, in hesitation, that through all her married life she had kept boarders to support the family and educate the children.

I could not go further and say that my father was such a poor business man that he could not even collect his bills. I might have given for him a historical justification. He was a survival from what I learned the economists had called the Barter stage of economic evolution. He could not fit himself to the Money and Credit economy. He was marvellous, I thought in my youthful days, at what in Indiana we called "swapping." He would come out with large accretions of "corporeal" property—farms, printing offices, horses, and the like. But he could not operate them on the money and credit system. Even when he was a harness-maker he neglected his shop, which he had acquired by swapping, and spent his time in writing articles and poetry and making pictures. I learned afterwards what it meant to have a wife who sacrificed a career for her children and her husband.

Although he never had more than a country school education, my father was a studious reader of Milton, Shakespeare, other poets, and of history. He was considered quite a literary genius around town, and when the Republicans started a local campaign sheet he was made its editor. He worked for nothing—that is, for love. It was this love of writing for a cause that led him to swap his harness shop and acquire his own paper, the *Union City Times*. Afterwards he made several trades and came out as owner of three hundred and sixty acres in the unsettled Red River Valley of Minnesota, thirty acres in the pine forests of Florida, and *The Winchester Herald* at the county seat. For a time he owned two newspapers, acquired by swapping, the one at Union City and the one at Winchester. He traded off the former. We moved to Winchester in 1878. It was in these country newspaper and job offices that my brother and I learned the printing trade, beginning at thirteen years of age, in vacations and out of school hours. This was an all-round education for us, which afterwards enabled us to piece out our mother's boarding-house earnings at Oberlin until I graduated in 1888, and my mother's health had gone.

My brother and I, seeing how the *Herald* was running down financially, worked up a scheme whereby we should take over the financial and mechanical work, leaving to father the editorial writing and news-gathering. After we moved to Winchester I collected, in Union City, some silver dollars out of hundreds owed to my father for advertising and subscriptions. This was my beginning in the money and credit economy. But he would not listen to our scheme. Eventually my mother, in 1882, seeing no future for her children and worrying about our falling in with bad associates, took her savings of $100 and sent me to Oberlin. She and the other two children followed the next year, after I had rented a shack of a house for keeping boarders. We were afraid to venture on a better house, but took this old unpainted one which the college was allowing to run down in expectation of tearing it down. She kept that place for more than ten years, using it latterly as a rooming house for indigent students. It was a very large house and her subrentals brought a small surplus, until my brother and I obtained jobs and were able to take care of father and mother until they died, both in the year 1895.

It was a pity to leave father alone at Winchester. He had had a paralytic stroke in one arm, from which he later recovered. But when the *Herald* no longer paid its way after we had gone, one of his Hoosier cronies, 'Gene Watson, took the paper off his hands for his eldest son, Seward, also a printer in our office. Seward made a success of the paper.

'Gene Watson was the father of James E. Watson who later, as Senator, served as the whip of the Republican party in Congress for many years. Indeed, in my high school days at Winchester my education was promoted, unknown to us, by two future eminent politicians in our part of the country, Senator Watson and Governor James P. Goodrich. Goodrich became, supposedly, a millionaire and then governor of Indiana. Watson became the most eloquent orator in the state, head of the Knights of St. Pythias, then United States Congressman and Senator. We debated in high school, dived in the old swimming hole, played seven-up under the apple tree, were members of the Republican Artillery Club that boomed the rallies of a pivotal state in honor of Robert Ingersoll, Senator Roscoe Conklin of New York, and the future President Benjamin Harrison. I carried the gun's ammunition. We separated when I was sent to Oberlin. We joined again at Madison in boyhood raillery when I was supporting Senator La Follette and they were wheel-horse stalwarts.

After father's sale of the *Winchester Herald* he came to Oberlin to live with us. For the first time, but after he was seventy years of age, I learned to know him. Like so many of the early rationalists of the Nineteenth Century, who had turned to spiritualism—as I later learned in my studies of labor history—my father had turned from Spencerism to spiritualism and then to Christian Science. His spiritualism came in Indiana after the death of my next brother, the best beloved of all their children by both Father and Mother. Father sought to find Frankie and his own younger sister, Elvira, in all the seances he could hear about anywhere in Indiana. His last word on his dying bed was "Elvira." His Christian Science came after he was seventy years old, and he brought to me several of the books of that faith which we happily read together. I had then gone far enough in college to trace his books back to Bishop Berkeley's idealism and missionary self-sacrifice in the early part of the Eighteenth Century. This information strongly fortified my father in this third version of Christianity, when he knew it was a religion nearly two centuries old, and doubtless much older. It was, in fact, his own Quaker pietism. Whatever others may say of Christian Science, I trace my father's to Bishop Berkeley, and I know that it made the last six or seven years of his life religious, healthful, and happy.

So the rift in my parents' home was bridged in their old age by two versions of Christianity. Both Mother and Father knew their Bible thoroughly from childhood. They came from two versions of Puritanism in the Seventeenth Century of England, the Presbyterians and Quakers, who, in that century were intolerant of each other. Mother relaxed her Calvinism when she thought of her children, two of whom died in childhood, and the others wandered away in looser beliefs. Father forgot his Spencerism when he sought his beloved Frankie, and still more when he had failed in worldly affairs and took to the pietism of Christian Science.

I look back now, in my own pensive inability to work, and try to find, in the historic versions of the Puritanism of Father and Mother, the bent that curved me through seventy years. Certainly, by heredity alone, I must have been a savage. Herein Calvin was right. For this reason my mother loved her second-born, Frankie, while she wept in secret and whipped her first-born. Frankie was a generous, loving child, who died at five years of age. The only time I ever saw tears in my mother's eyes was when I came in from clubbing to death with a pump handle a mangy dog, surrounded by the awe-struck younger children in the "alley." I remember how I calmly hit Frankie on the head with a hatchet. I wonder if modern child psychology finds all children original sinners. Certainly it was not so with my brother Frankie, though it was so with me. I remember my first assertion of independence, aged seven. I refused to cry when Mother whipped me, and I insisted that my curls should be cut off. My elder half-sister, Anna, had been curling them twice a week. But one day I came home from the barber and handed them to her. She took them with tears and has preserved two of them to this day. Now, many years a widow, she lives with me at eighty-six years of age while I am seventy-one. She is a full-blooded Quaker, I am a hybrid of Quaker and Presbyterian. I must have been a beauty covering a savage. The first time I remember any show of affection was at twelve, when Anna was married and took the night train for Erie, Pennsylvania. I cried myself to sleep.

But my salvation came when my mother sent me to Oberlin, aged twenty. For twenty years thereafter I did not smoke or drink, though I must say the first three months were terrible in giving up my surreptitious pipe.

At Oberlin my brother and I learned the difference between union and non-union printing offices. When we first went to Oberlin we set type in the local office at ten cents an hour. I also had picked up wood engraving without any teacher, at the printing office in Indiana. During my first three months at Oberlin I did about $100 of work, making pictures of wagons for an unfortunate establishment just starting at Winchester. This figured out at one dollar per hour. I tried to get into a large wood-engraving establishment at Cleveland, but they thought my wagons did not show any contrast in shading. Then I saw an item in a paper of the new invention of photo-engraving. So I escaped technological unemployment, and stuck to type-setting. That was not displaced by the linotype until ten years later, when I had become a teacher.

Our local printing office at Oberlin ran a daily paper

during commencement season. They brought down from Cleveland a former Oberlin printer as foreman. He found that I was the fastest type-setter in the office. I think this was because I always started painfully slow in the morning, so as not to miss a letter or make any false motion. Then, after an hour or two, my hand was flying around the "case" in curves, while the others were jabbing and missing. This was an empirical time-and-motion study. I did not know until fifteen years later that it could be elevated into a science of management.

Anyhow, Sidney Leonard, our imported foreman, invited me to come to Cleveland, and promised to get me into the union as a "sub" on the *Cleveland Herald.* I went, and began setting type the first night as a substitute for an absentee printer. I did this for four summers, leaving Oberlin before commencement and remaining until a week or two before the fall opening.

My brother came during the second summer and got a "sub" job across the street in a non-union office. He and I had been setting type together in the Oberlin office. There we had made a contract with the local publisher to take over the mechanical work on the students' paper, the *Oberlin Review,* which appeared bi-weekly. We got jointly $15.00 for the two weeks, $7.50 per week, which we turned over to Mother. After the first year the publisher discovered that we were making too much money —about twice as much as his hourly rate of ten cents. He refused to renew the contract and put us back on the hour-rate.

At Cleveland we were paid piece rates, the same rate on both daily papers. But we had to work about eleven or twelve hours a day, three hours in the afternoon distributing type to the cases without pay, and eight or nine hours at night until about four o'clock in the morning, on a rate of thirty-five cents per thousand "ems." By working seven nights a week I could earn about $20.00 per week, though the average run of the office was about $15.00 per week. But this included, in our union office, an equal distribution of the "fat" which went to the foreman's "pets" in the non-union office. I took a hand at the fat. The "father of the chapel" held an auction every three months. The "fat" was the advertising, baseball scores, and anything that paid more than the regular rate. My first bid on the baseball scores was ten per cent of my gross receipts on that work. This amount was distributed by the "father" to the other printers. But I made several labor-saving, or rather labor-enlarging, devices. I went to the saloons before working hours and took off the ball-scores which did not usually get to us from the editorial room before eleven o'clock at night. So the boys put up a job on me at the next auction. They, too, thought I was earning too much money and was not a real workingman anyhow. They forced me, by a set-up bidding against me, to put up my bid to forty-two per cent. This, I found, took all or more of the fat, and I had my extra saloon-work and overtime ball-scores for nothing. Yet, by this distribution of all the fat in the office, each of us got one to three dollars per week above our earnings at regular rates.

Thus I learned what was the meaning of collective action in control of individual action. Fifty years afterwards I named it an "institution," and extended it, as a part of economic science, to all corporations, trade associations, banks, and every occupation. To me it has always been something vivid, even painful; but I learned to look upon it philosophically as the way in which rights, duties, liberties and exposures are created in the relations of the individual to society. My only rights and liberties in type-setting were created by that little society of printers and had been administered, since the gilds of the Middle Ages, by the "father of the chapel." Other unions, without this ancient religion, have only materialistic "shop chairmen," "walking delegates," or "business agents." But I am an honorary member, since 1891, of Typographical No. 53, Cleveland, Ohio, where I got my first lesson in the religion of the Middle Ages, in their patron saints, and in economic justice. By working ten weeks the first summer and boarding in a workingman's home—where I got into bed at 4 A.M. with a hairy monster who had gone to bed naked and half-drunk—I remember bringing $200 home to Mother. When my brother came, the second summer, we boarded ourselves by means of a big steam cooker that got our dinner and midnight lunch in the afternoon while we distributed type at the printing office.

Fifteen years afterwards I visited the old office, now the *Cleveland Plain Dealer*. I found six men instead of our thirty, publishing a paper twice as large at three cents instead of five, weekly wages three times as high, hours reduced to eight, afternoon distribution cut out—all because the national president of our typographical union, Samuel Donnelly, in 1895, my friend in later years, made an agreement with the Mergenthaler Linotype Company to welcome and install the machine wherever union members were given a preference and six months to learn the machine. Non-union newspaper offices copied the union schedule. I often contrast with my students this union negotiation in the printing trade with the destruction of the union in the steel industry at the Homestead strike of 1892. No wonder I have always avowed my philosophy of trade unionism.

How strange is Memory! Some forty years after my type-setting days, when I was lecturing at the summer school for lawyers at Yale University, I walked at night with a lawyer student along the streets of New Haven. We came to a daily newspaper office. I bragged to the foreman and linotype operators that I was a union printer. To remove their doubts I boasted that, though I had not touched a type for nearly forty years, I could set up my name for them from an old "case" which I saw nearby. They gathered around. I was staggered at first when I looked at the case, with its hundred boxes of letters. I could not remember the location of a single letter of the alphabet. I had to ask where the "cap J" was, passing it off as one of the curiosities handed down from ancient times when the caps J and U were added at the end of the alphabet after the early cap case had been laid out in alphabetic order. They pointed to the J box. I picked up a J, and immediately, without thinking, I knew where the O was, and when I got the O I knew where the H was, and so on without mistake. The printers proudly stereotyped my set-up and I handed out my business card to each of them. Intellectually I knew nothing. Unconsciously I knew only where the next letter was. I never studied psychology except with my Oberlin professor who ridiculed the "knee jerk." I missed the subject at Johns Hopkins where I intended to study with Stanley Hall, but he, unknown to me, had gone to inaugurate Clark University. All I know is accidental experiments like this one of remembrance after forty years. But I found eventually, after reading C. S. Peirce, the founder of Pragmatism, that it reversed the mechanistic and intellectualistic psychology of the economists from Bentham to the Twentieth Century, which I had started to teach. My forty years' interval between type-setting gave to me my own firm foundation in pragmatic psychology for my later *Institutional Economics* of past, present, future, habit and custom.

At Oberlin, in 1887, my mother and I started an anti-saloon publication. It was at the beginning of the Anti-Saloon League, of which Howard H. Russell, then a theological student at Oberlin, became, for more than forty years, the national organizer. Our League was a non-partisan organization, intending to bring about prohibition of the liquor traffic by local option, and therefore opposed to the Prohibition party and the movement to get national prohibition through the Republican party. I set the type on our anti-saloon publication and printed in it my "Junior Exhibition" speech on local-option as against my opponent who argued for national prohibition. The speech pleased an Oberlin audience, including my mother, who could not bear to see the Republican party weakened. I had cast my first vote, in 1884, for St. John, the Prohibitionist candidate for President of the United States, against the passionate protests of my mother and brother. I was "throwing my vote away." Here I began my fifty-year record of voting for third parties. Only after seventy years of age do I refuse to endorse third-party movements.

Ten or twelve years after my first venture I even voted,
at Syracuse, for the candidate of the Communists for
governor of New York, because I did not like the Republican and Democratic state political machines, and I knew
the candidate. At any rate the Anti-Saloon League pushed
forward its local option campaign until it became state
option and then, during the War, national prohibition,
without a third party. Always this program relieved both
the Republican and the Democratic politicians from the
predicament of declaring themselves on a moral issue.

I was not unaware of the devious windings even of local
option. In Florida they had county option. Leesburg was
in a "dry" county; the next county was "wet." The boys
in the Leesburg printing office, where I worked in the
winter of 1885-86, imported each Saturday from the next
county a glass gallon can of "coal oil." We devoted ourselves Saturday night and Sunday, in the printing office, to
a friendly consumption of this imported gin, and to plug-
cutting our own smoking tobacco according to the Southern fashion. We operated a small-scale coöperative boot-
legging fraternity in the printing office.

I should mention that this Florida year was an excep-
tion to my above pious claim of abstinence for twenty
years from drinking and smoking. It figures down differently. To make the whole thing more scientific, I mark off
my cycles of alcho-tobaccism, first, from thirteen to twenty
years of age, a peak of surreptitious luxury; then, twenty
to thirty-eight years of age, a depression and trough, except for the year in Florida; then, thirty-eight to seventy-
one years of age a curve upwards, skewed somewhat by
national prohibition, home manufacture, and occasional

boot-legging. And now, at seventy-one, just as the whole nation turns wet and smokes cigarettes, my stomach gets mad again and I am painfully soothing it by trying to go dry and smokeless. It is a lot to pay for a happy old age.

Indeed it is hopeless. So I construct experimentally a stabilizing scheme which I devised by comparing Northern and Southern business men. In 1906, when investigating municipal ownership for the National Civic Federation, I was put up at the Jefferson Club in Richmond, Virginia. I noticed that the business men came in at noon and lit up at the Club bar, after which they lunched voluminously. This was different from my observations on Wall Street, either on the top-floor café of the Federal Reserve bank, or in the Railroad Club or neighboring places. There the financiers, whether millionaires or clerks, might nibble at a bar of chocolate and drink only fizz water. I asked, Why? They said it was the same with them at breakfast. They would have a strenuous forenoon and afternoon on the Stock Exchange or in the banks or commercial houses, and must keep their brains clear. But at night, Oh My! cocktails, champagne, a glorious dinner! I learned that Northern business men did not get drunk until nightfall when their business was finished for the day. But Southern business men began at noon, between business hours. So my present scheme of stabilization copies the Northerners in the forenoon and the Southerners in the afternoon. I do it by advancing my dinner hour from night to noon. I work and read and study in the forenoon, beginning about 4 A.M., on the Northern plan. I eat and drink at noon but loaf and sleep and trim trees and take my hot baths in the afternoon. I do not say that this scheme would fit everybody above seventy years of age. It is my private scheme which again conciliates North and South in my own person.

How curiously I reversed my time schedule of fifty years ago. In the daily newspaper office I worked till four o'clock in the morning and then slept till noon. Likewise, in my Oberlin and Johns Hopkins days and my early teaching days I worked as late at night as I could keep awake. But, in my interval, after leaving Syracuse, I spent two and a half hours per day on the transportation system of New York. I left home about seven in the morning and returned about seven at night. I saw nothing of my children. So my wife began to keep them up till I returned. I played with them, made pictures for them, put them to bed at nine, and went to bed at nine myself. They could sleep until eight in the morning, but I could sleep only until four or five. So I began my day's work in my study at these early morning hours. When we moved to Madison I saved two hours per day in transportation between home and office. In this way I could study and write three or four hours before breakfast while the others were asleep. By force of parental circumstance I had adopted the agricultural schedule, early to bed, early to rise. This reversal of my time schedule has made possible the genesis of my ideas.

But I had to have something to keep me going in these pre-prandial hours. I turned to coffee and smoking. I made the coffee one-fourth strength. My housekeeper calls it slop. I don't mind offensive names. They have fitted my time schedule for forty years.

In a period of despondency after first coming to Madi-

son, I changed from coffee to whisky. Thereby I certainly
had floods of brilliant ideas in those early mornings, all
by myself. But they were ideas created by the circulation
of alcohol, not the circulation of blood. So I sobered back
to feeble coffee in the early morning hours.

These physiological details may seem foreign to a book
on the evolution of my ideas. But I find that they appeal
to my Friday Niters. I take them into the secrets of my
animal life. They see that I am human. My Friday Niters
include present husbands and wives as well as future husbands and wives. Indeed I long since became something of
a marriage bureau. Both sides of the clientele seem to be
interested. It is the method by which the wife converts
Nature's chemistry into professors' ideas—their own
new science of Home Economics.

I remember that my Hoosier father smoked and chewed
continuously, but did not drink, from thirteen to seventy.
Then he went total abstinence and Christian Science. All
Hoosiers chewed, but I never chewed tobacco but once,
and that was when I was off on a truant expedition from
school. I spent the time with my head down over a little
creek while the other boys went on and left me. I quit
chewing forever thereafter.

My father had saved, from the wreck of 1884, his thirty
acres in the pine forests of Florida and a hundred copies
of Kendall's horse-cure pamphlet which he had taken in
trade for advertising. The Florida pines were held because my mother paid the taxes. The three hundred and
sixty acres in the Red River Valley had been traded for
a printing office. The Kendall horse books were brought
to Oberlin because my brother and I thought we might ex-

change them with farmers for meals, if we decided to go on a "tramp." This we started to do in 1885, carrying them over our shoulders as we footed the railway tracks or stole a ride in front of the baggage car. But not a horse-book could we trade or sell or give away. So we slept in haymows and rifled the farmers' corn for roasting ears. The books got heavy and by stages we buried them without a sigh along the railroad track.

All of this came about because in the spring of 1885 I had my first nervous breakdown. Coming out from a Greek examination, a fierce blow from outside seemed to hit inside my head. I could hardly walk home. Then I spent three months wandering through the woods about Oberlin, until the end of the school year. My brother, Alvin, previously, when our funds were running low, had generously left Oberlin looking for a job, leaving my sister and me to continue our studies. At the end of the school year I also started on a hike and joined him at Au Sable, a sawdust town in Northern Michigan on Lake Huron, where he had found a job in a printing office. Never after, at Oberlin, was I able to finish up a school year. When it came to graduation, in 1888, the faculty permitted me to take oral "make-up" examinations, which the dear professors said were "poor," but none would stand in the way of my graduation.

My collegiate record was indeed bad, and cut me out from the traditional honors, such as Phi Beta Kappa which many others got. I think my professors saw some promise, not in my scholarship but in my curiosity and persistency; or they saw some alleviation in my poor health.

I fell behind in my Greek class because I insisted on hunting up everything I could find on the letter Omega. I fell behind in biology because I persisted in finding the heartbeat of a little red water-bug that came to life before the ice was out, in the roadside ditches. The other students went on with the regular schedule of specimens. But I stuck stubbornly to that little bug. Yet I never could verify the pictures I saw in the scientific publications which my friendly professor finally hunted up for me. I became skeptical of scientists. That piece of stubborn curiosity, I think, gave me a "pass" at the end of the course, for otherwise I failed on the examination. It was all I ever knew, from my own investigation, in biology. Afterwards, in economics, it took me more than twenty-five years after 1907 to work out persistently, by numerous mistakes, the transition from the economists' concept of "exchange" to the legal-economic concept of a "transaction."

I had had previously a similar experience—at nineteen years of age—after graduating from high school, when I was a failure in teaching a country school near Winchester. In passing the country slaughterhouse, on my four-mile walk once a week from Winchester to the school, I would get the butcher to give me an ox's heart, or eye, or some other piece of anatomy, to demonstrate to the pupils the pictures found in our textbook. But we never could identify a single valve or layer of muscle or anything else which we found so plainly pictured in the book. The pupils lost faith in me, tumbled me in the grass, pelted me with snow balls, and I had to resign in three months. They wanted something "for sure," handed down by the great authorities of the past, and I couldn't produce it. I vowed that never again would I teach.

Then, in the middle of that winter, 1881, I saw the alluring advertisement for agents to sell the *Christian Union,* Henry Ward Beecher, editor. I was to go to Indianapolis for a week's intensive training in salesmanship. The literature and lectures they gave me there were exciting. I saw myself making untold dollars per week, by mere personality. Then I started out, hiking in snow and rain and mud. Never a subscription did I take. "Henry Ward" was suspect by the women and his religion uninteresting to the men. I was a cold, wet failure. Ever since have I been skeptical of advertisers and salesmanship. "They say" salesmanship has now become a science. I think my experiment was as scientific as my later struggles with Omega and the Little Bug. Disillusioned within four months by advertisers, scientists, and teachers, at the age of nineteen, I decided to become a journalist, and went back to my father's printing office.

I had read in the printing office at Leesburg, Florida, in the year 1885-86, that Herbert Spencer had recently maintained that, according to the science of physics, it was impossible to pitch a curved ball. He knew not the seams on the ball and forgot the friction of the air. His was evidently a single-track mind. Ever after, I looked for the omitted factors, or the ones taken for granted and therefore omitted, by the great leaders in the science of economics. That was how I became an economic skeptic.

My brother and I experimented on Spencer's omitted factors, with our log house as backstop. I learned all four

curves. When I returned to Oberlin in April, 1886, the
baseball season was on. The seniors, my former classmates, were sweeping everything. My brilliant friend, Job
Fish, was their pitcher. He could get his lessons in a third
of the time it took me, and then gave the rest of the time
to preparing me for recitations. His was a huge muscular
frame and he could throw a straight ball like a cannon.
Nobody, it seems, had ever heard of a curved ball. The
catcher on the junior side discovered my twisters. He
made the signs to me. The slow up-curve did the business.
Job Fish got the only "out" that I pitched. It came straight
to me like a thunderbolt. Somehow, unconsciously, from
boyhood habit, I reached out my left hand and held it. I
could not use that hand for two weeks. My friend, the
catcher, did not make the "out" sign to me again. He
stuck to the "up" sign, though my "ups" were slow. Nobody got to first base in the first eight innings. The score
stood 7 to 0 in our favor. Then Job got mad. He quit
throwing over the base and threw at me. Certainly he
rattled me when I came to the bat. He hit me on the side
of the head, adjoining the temple. Evidently I was not an
all-round ball player. My playing was academic, like
Herbert Spencer's theory. I had not learned to dodge
straight lightning. I insisted on pitching the ninth inning.
But the boys of my own team physically held me down.
They took me to the doctor. He encouraged us all by
saying that such a blow did not usually show its results
until ten years later. They forced me to bed, where my
indigestion returned for a week. My substitute pitcher,
Harry Brown, afterwards chaplain to Roosevelt's Rough
Riders, could not, by his straight ball, keep the seniors

from making ten runs in the ninth inning. But the Athletic Association held a mass-meeting that afternoon. They voted Job unanimously out of baseball forever.

Ten years later I had a letter from Job, then a high official with the Otis Elevator Company. He wrote that he had been worrying about me these ten years, but seeing that I was not yet dead, or insane, he must tell me how ashamed and glad he was. We returned to our good friendship. Poor fellow, he died within a year or two, and here I am, forty years after the doctor's allotted ten years, though with the same indigestion.

I never played baseball again.

In this old age of mine I began to brag about pitching the first curved ball in America. I was able to get away with it on a visit to Oberlin, where I was currying favor with the students to listen to my lecture on political economy. There were two witnesses on the faculty who got up and testified. They had seen the game. Then I tried to brag it out, in Madison, on my fifty-year-old Town and Gown Club. One member figured out that he had seen a curved ball in 1884. Therefore, I was the first at Oberlin but not the first in America. So it is ever thus. I may do something stunning or unexpected, but, if so, I soon drop out because somebody else does it better or has already done it. I have found my most brilliant thoughts anticipated long before, in my study of earlier economists in the original.

Return to the thirty acres in Florida. My mother financed that project also. She had an extra supply of girl boarders in Oberlin that year, 1885, in a better house around the corner. She kept the old house for roomers.

My brother was setting type in Michigan. I could neither study nor set type. I managed to get back to Winchester, where my brother-in-law, George Best, and my elder sister, Anna, had taken the old home of three acres on the edge of town. George was traveling for the Standard Oil Company. He came across a second-hand steam incubator. He brought it to Winchester. I started hatching chickens. I had to sit up most of the night watching the temperature gage on that supposedly automatic incubator. But I brought out two hundred chicks. Now I was in for it, giving my mind a rest. I put in another batch of eggs and built brooders for the first two hundred. The fluffy chicks were enticing at night as they sprawled out full length on the warm sand of my brooders, quite like a flock of baby sheep. Then the second batch came out. More brooders. I learned that animal language is not hereditary. It is customary. The first brood came to me when I clucked, the second brood when I whistled. Neither came to me on the other's language. All of them ran under me when it rained, and I squatted down to catch them and toss them into the brooder pens. They converted me into a mother hen. This was hereditary. The family and neighbors came over to see me function. I was getting back to Nature. My nerves and digestion were restored. Probably there survived two hundred broilers when I left for Florida in October. The fatality was immense. I was not Nature's hen. The survivors I suppose George sold and, being a salesman, I suppose he sold the incubator.

In Florida my father and brother had preceded me. They built a log house and rived logs for a paling fence.

I turned in, cutting the tall hard-wood pines. We made railway ties and sold them at the nearby railway station at ten cents apiece. The town, Wildwood, was two miles away and the county seat, Leesburg, ten miles away. We were in the primeval forest, the center of Florida. Our nearest neighbors were one or two miles away, calling themselves "Georgia Crackers." In them we found the original Hoosiers and could talk their language. We differed only on one thing, and that was not really a difference: "You-uns overwhelmed us—you didn't conquer us." We agreed to that.

When our money began to run out, Brother and I started on a tramp. He washed dishes in Jacksonville and Palatka hotels but finally landed in a printing office at Tavares, about twenty miles from our thirty acres. I found a printing job immediately at Leesburg, ten miles away. Every Sunday we walked half-way each, on the railway track, to have a beautiful visit. We sent our money to Father. When we got back we found he had bought a flock of chickens, possible in his Indiana, but impossible in Florida. We were mad and not respectful to his old age. We turned in again to clearing ten acres out of the thirty, planting orange trees, and when the turnips came up in February, we never ate anything as good as turnip greens. We had lived the winter on beans and pork, with an occasional fresh beef brought through the woods by a "cracker." Brother and I had boarded ourselves when in the Cleveland printing offices. I fixed up a bed on the floor in the Leesburg office. My dog was a help. He brought in sweet potatoes, bananas, oranges, from the groceries, a package of money-orders from the post office, old shoes and leather for the shoemaker whose shop was on the same floor as the type-setting room. It was the second floor of the courthouse. The printing presses, including a cylinder press and a steam engine, were in the basement. I found that I was an all-round printer, from setting type to running the press and stoking the engine, thanks to my father's printing office in Indiana. I was soon made foreman. A deaf and dumb fellow printer, previously on the job, came to the "devil" in the basement and excitedly drew his finger across his throat, pointing up to me. I had displaced him in the line of seniority. The devil told me. Thereafter I carried a gun. Such are the dangers of promotion on the frontier.

It was a romantic life and the happiest I have known. I have told my Friday Niters stories of "crackers" and their bananas, Negro hunts, Negroes brought in dead to our courthouse, or slashing each other at Christmas with razors and filling the gaps with Spanish moss; of revolvers we carried, of branded cows, razor-back hogs, pine-tree squirrels bigger than cats, huge crocodiles and snakes in the swamps and shallow lakes, coon hunts with the crackers—it was a poetic pine-roofed sanitarium for nerves. When I returned to Oberlin in April, 1886, I met a stranger approaching me in the narrow aisle of the sleeping car. I stepped aside, but he stepped just the same. It was myself, weighing one hundred and sixty pounds. The highest I had reached before had been one hundred and twenty. Now, in 1934, it is one hundred and four to one hundred and ten.

But my father and brother were not so fortunate. They stayed on and got malaria. My younger sister went down to be with them but returned immediately. My father came home on his back. Interior Florida was no place for Northerners after April. My brother was always sore on me for leaving them. It happened because I suddenly learned of a sick Northerner and his wife leaving Florida for Cincinnati, and needing a companion. The Northerner died at Atlanta and his wife and I brought him to Cincinnati in a coffin. My mother traded our Florida orange grove for a town lot in Oberlin, and sold the lot for $500.

Forty-eight years afterwards, in 1933, I went to Florida again, weighing one hundred and four, this time financed by my Friday Niters. I went in April to Sarasota on the Gulf Coast, south of Tampa, and basked dishabille on the sand. I could find only one man who had lived in Florida before I lived there, forty-eight years before. He owned land in Sarasota, some of which he sold to Northerners in the boom period; they are now mostly bankrupt with empty skyscrapers taller than the few remaining pines. He was living fine, fat, and lazy, a parvenu cracker in a colony of Northern millionaires.

I hunted for the location in Tampa of the old printing office where I set type in 1885. What I found was a huge marble interior on the ground floor of a skyscraper. The other day I listened to a broadcast of the Tampa Carnival and State Fair, coming from the roof of that building. In Tampa I did not speak to anybody. The romance had gone. Tampa, for me, was a sprawling Spanish village of cigarmakers, with a big sandy square, a town pump, and a watchman singing, "Midnight and all's well!" Tampa now boasted 150,000 population and towering buildings that I had seen aplenty and even bigger. But I came back in a month, weighing one hundred and fourteen.

In my days at Oberlin and Cleveland I saw the beginnings of this marvellous technological age. I blunderingly used the first telephone from Oberlin to Cleveland. I saw the beginnings of photo-engraving. I saw, at Cleveland, the first electric street car shooting flashes of lightning from its underground trolley. The first carbon light shed down a moonlight from skeleton towers, seventy feet above, to the streets of Cleveland below. We changed from gas light to long blue incandescent tubes over our cases in the printing office, which bewildered the type-setters rebelliously. Afterwards came Edison's carbon bulbs.

Other technological changes came in rapidly during the next fifty years. I judge myself now, at seventy-one, not by brains, but by avoirdupois. I have installed a weighing machine in my bathroom. There I have set up a home sanitarium with ideas I brought from Harrogate, the English Carlsbad, where the money of my Friday Niters financed me in 1933. I think all homes for workingmen should be built around a home sanitarium. For there have I imported and improved on Florida by means of General Electric ultra-violet rays and fuel oil pumped by electricity generated thirty miles away by the Wisconsin River. I bask in a nudist retreat of my own, in my sanitarium at any hour, day, night, rain or snow, and in the sunny summer on my shrub-surrounded lawn, looking down one hundred and ten feet on Mendota, which itself, I am told, looks from my window like the Bay of Naples. Six miles across the lake before me I watch the white caps or mirror glass, the creeping cloud shadows or deep blue from a cloudless sky. Fifteen miles away I see the sky-line which I can imagine is the Rockies fifty miles away. Fifty feet from me are my waving blue spruce which I planted twenty years ago. My V-8 Ford, bought with what was left of my Friday Niters' money after trips to Florida and England, takes me five miles to Madison and the University in ten minutes, where my horse and buggy, including the nuisance of harnessing and unharnessing, hitching and unhitching, required sixty minutes. Airplanes go alarmingly fifty feet above my house, and New York and my sister, a thousand miles away, are twenty hours instead of three days for our letters. I listen to wireless, the most astounding of all, which brings to me Roosevelt in Washington, Admiral Byrd in the Antarctic and the Farmers' Home Hour. More than a dozen variabilities of electricity operate my home, from curling hair to washing the clothes which I washed in a tub for my mother in my childhood days. No more traveling or work for me. Wave-lengths instead. I trim trees in my orchard for fun, instead of playing golf, which had become work instead of fun. The new technological age brings the world and the sun to me at my bidding in my hill-top home. I return in a second childhood where I began in the first. I bring the South, by technology, to me in the North, where, seven decades ago, heredity brought the South and the North together in me. I myself am a revolution out of a wave-length revolution about me which I have witnessed through fifty years. And yet, there are millions unemployed and distressed who are forbidden to enter. Is it Satan's joke? Anyhow, I must go on.

The Supreme Court says the present state of the nation is an Emergency. But what is an emergency in a world of ceaseless change? It is only a speeding up or slowing down of the velocity. I have lived through the highest velocity known to mankind. I have seen it speed up and slow down. At last I find refuge with my daughter Rachel who takes care of me and who, returning from the desert West, writes for me her version of the retired cowboy:

I never need roam
From my bright, hill-top home,
Where the sunbeams and soft shadows play;
Where the silvery sheen
Of the Lake can be seen,
And I've peace and contentment all day.

Far, far from the strife
Of Man's turbulent life,
I rest on my quiet, domed hill;
Where pain I forget,
Where hope lingers yet,
And the heartaches I knew are quite still.

Home! Home on my hill!
Where the sunbeams and soft shadows play;
Where the silvery sheen
Of the Lake can be seen,
And I've peace and contentment all day!

III

GRADUATE AND TEACHER

WHEN I was graduated at Oberlin by the indulgence of my professors, in 1888, aged twenty-six, I looked healthy enough. My modern daughter, specializing in anthropology, now tells me that, compared with my twelve and seventy-one, I looked "sensuous." In my mother's generation a friend wrote to her that I looked "verve." Whichever it was, I thereafter was able to get through with two years at the university and several years of teaching. I learned through the years that it was not the athletic, brilliant, weighty classmates who held out the longest. They needed not take care of themselves. It was the little, frail fellows, with headaches and afraid or unable to eat too much. It was not health that kept me going—it was the warnings of a mad stomach and a neurotic brain. I learned, by forty years of age, not to work after these organs sent their signals to my solar plexus. I discovered that I was just an animal, but I could take a hint in time.

It was my dear Professor Monroe, at Oberlin, who helped me to go to Johns Hopkins University. Recently he had come to Oberlin, with white hair, as Professor of Political Science and Modern History, after some thirty years in public life as a representative from the Western Reserve at Washington with Joshua Giddings, Ben Wade,

SELF, 26, 1888

and James A. Garfield. This had been followed by a con-
sulship at Rio Janeiro. When he told us about his experiences it was thrilling. When he prayed, as all did at the
opening of classes, it was a familiar conversation with
God. His public life had made him tolerant of the contradictory opinions of others. In my first year at Oberlin,
1882, I had read George's *Progress and Poverty,* recommended to me there by a good old fellow printer. In my
senior year I joined with other students to organize the
Henry George Club. We brought George himself to
Oberlin for a public lecture, well attended but strongly
resisted from the floor. Harry Weld and I asked Professor Monroe to let us have four days of his time to lecture
on George. Harry took the deductive God-given rights of
man to the land. I took the statistics, mainly from Thomas
G. Shearman. It was all directly contrary to our Professor's
Republican party and protectionism. The only criticism he
made was against calling our club by the name of a man.
We should get a broader name based on our principles.
This was the politician's correct insight, but we had not
then heard of the name "single tax," latterly changed to
"welfare taxation." So we let it go at Henry George.

Afterwards I attended all the single-tax clubs wherever
I happened to be. Yet I was a convinced protectionist
from father, mother, and Professor Monroe. My trade-
union, too, was contradictory to Henry George, and I did
not like his attack on labor unions in his book. Neither did
I like his shifting of taxes to the farmers' fertility of the
soil which he and the single taxers thought was God-
given, whereas I, agreeing with Ricardo, could see that it
was mostly man-made. Thirty-five years after our lectures

in Professor Monroe's class I drafted a bill for a farmer single-tax member of the Wisconsin legislature, exempting fertility and taxing only site-values. Harry Weld and other members of our Henry George Club had abandoned the theory altogether, but I stuck to reducing it to whatever might be true and workable. For this I had been roundly attacked, when on the Industrial Relations Commission of 1915, by the single-taxers as selling out to the capitalists. I changed the meaning of "value" from George's version of Ricardo's "cost of production" to Henry C. Carey's "opportunity-value," and thus exempted the farmers' fertility of the soil. The bill, in 1923, was characterized by opponents as a "farmers' single tax," because it won over all the dirt-farmers in the legislature, whereas farmers were always indignantly opposed to Henry George's transfer of taxes to land-values, including the value of fertility. This revision of single-tax theory I afterwards incorporated in my book on institutional economics, making it a derivation from the American judge-made law of special assessments and police-power.

But Professor Monroe was tolerant of our youthful doctrinairism. It was in my junior year that I decided to give up journalism and go to Johns Hopkins University for political economy. The idea came from my Japanese friend, Toyokichi Iyenaga, who graduated in 1887. He was going to Johns Hopkins. I had also seen an editorial attack on Professor Ely, in *The Nation,* for his so-called socialism. This augmented my desire to go to Johns Hopkins. Iyenaga won the oratorical contest at Oberlin. I helped him to put on a public lecture on the Revolution of 1868 in Japan, which yielded him a hundred dollars or so for his graduate work. He and I then put on a summer lecture course in the towns around Oberlin. I was advance agent, in a plug hat and a twelve-dollar suit of clothes. I operated the stereopticon. This trip was a failure. It left my mother in the hole ninety dollars, which Iyenaga repaid later in Baltimore. For he had become a Chautauqua lecturer, with headquarters ultimately at Chicago University. Years later he made a horseback survey of "agriculture" for the Japanese Government in Korea, Formosa, and parts of China. Still later, Iyenaga became éditor of Japanese propaganda in America from New York.

Professor Monroe set about to finance me for Johns Hopkins. He induced two of the trustees of Oberlin College to lend me the money during two years. My only security was a life insurance policy of $1,000. On one of my notes of $500 I paid ten per cent because the lender, Mr. Albert H. Johnson, one of the Oberlin trustees, was paying that rate for loans on his railway in Arkansas. On the other note the lender, Mr. William Sumner, also a trustee of Oberlin, when it came to paying up, declined interest charges. It took me fourteen years to pay these notes, with accrued interest, after I had become an investigator for the United States Industrial Commission.

I never afterwards learned how to keep out of debt. Debts had given me a wonderful graduate education. Always my wife and I wanted to own a home with a mortgage on it. This was different from a life insurance policy, which is not foreclosed until death. We sold the homes at a total loss when we so frequently moved elsewhere. I became doubtful about workingmen owning their homes. Unemployment and moving about dissolve the alluring visions painted by real estate dealers. From childhood I knew the meaning of thrift. It meant keeping boarders instead of borrowing. Working long hours for the future is one's own physical thrift. Borrowing is a dangerous use of other people's money. I never could get rid of debts. I finally made debts, instead of liberty, a foundation of Institutional Economics.

When I went to Baltimore, in 1888, I resolved to abandon all the theories of political economy which I had ever picked up, and to start, as John Locke would say, with a sheet of white paper. Within a year and a half came my usual fate. I failed completely on a history examination. This ruined my hopes of a fellowship to carry me through the third year. So I had only two years of graduate work and never reached the degree of Ph.D., the sign manual of a scholar. Afterwards I occasionally said to my students that, if I could have my way, there would be no examinations, no marks nor degrees in colleges and universities, because they gave preference to memorizers who could hand back what their teachers and textbooks said, and penalized independent thinking. But I could not spread that doctrine convincingly because I kept thinking I was that fox which had lost his tail. My degrees came as honorary degrees, M.A. and LL.D. from Oberlin, LL.D. from Lake Forest and Wisconsin, the last in 1931.

But at Johns Hopkins I learned a lot about political economy. I had always supposed that political economy was a deductive science of economic theory. Even Professor Monroe's lectures and his thirty years' experience, I took to be, as he did, excursions away from economics into political science. His protectionism was on the defensive against the orthodox free-trade theories of the economists. He appealed to history or his experience, and never pretended to teach us economics, though he used the standard textbook. My Henry George economics was only an extension of Ricardo's rent and free-trade. But Professor Ely set me at work visiting the building and loan associations in Baltimore, and joining the Charity Organization Society as a "case worker." I made reports on these subjects to the joint history and economics seminar, and one of them was published briefly in a University bulletin, a copy of which I sent to my mother.

The head of the charity organization society was John M. Glenn, afterwards for many years director of the Russell Sage Foundation, which financed my work with others on the Pittsburgh Survey in 1906-07. My assignment in case work at Baltimore was an old Civil War veteran on the Northern side. He was down with tuberculosis in the third story of a rattle-shack tenement, his wife doing all she could to care for him. He never had been able to get a pension. So I put in a year getting a pension for him. I got an insight, for the first time, of practical politics. I visited the pension office, interviewed lawyers, attached myself to the Democratic congressman from Baltimore where the sympathies were with the Confederate soldiers. I got the pension. Was this political economy?

Afterwards, when sociology was separated from political economy in university teaching, charity was transferred to sociology. I never could reconcile myself to this separation. I taught "sociology" at Syracuse University and got out a book in 1895 on machine politics, which was to be cured, I thought, by proportional representation. I

ended four years at Syracuse with a series of articles on
"A Sociological View of Sovereignty." A critic surprised
me by naming the articles An Economic View of Sovereignty. It became for me eventually Institutional Economics.

Then, again, I was, for one year, president of the Wisconsin Conference of Social Work, although the position
belonged to a sociologist. So I always thought that both
political science and sociology were branches of political
economy. I broke over without compunction into those
departments, when they were separated from economics
in the teaching curriculum.

At any rate, in 1888, my letters to my mother were flam-
ing with enthusiasm over this "new" political economy. It
was my tribute to her longing that I should become a minister of the Gospel. I brought her to Baltimore with me
the second year, where we had a lovely life and I was a
social worker as well as a graduate student in economics.

There, too, I budded into an assistant to Professor Ely,
at ten cents an hour, helping him on his first *Outlines of
Economics,* for Chautauqua courses. For this I got much
credit, more important than money, since he acknowledged my help in his preface, though, of my contributions, he used only two pages on liquor consumption. The
rest was miscellaneous, though I wrote up many kinds of
things which he did not use, but they were all inspired by
his new economics. He let me teach his John Stuart Mill
course for three weeks when he was out of town. But the
boys floored me and I considered myself a disaster.

I could not understand, in the summer of 1890, after
two years of graduate work, why my Baltimore teachers

recommended me to an instructorship in economics at Wesleyan University. I had failed in examinations and in getting a fellowship to finance the third year. The instructorship at Wesleyan was a relief at $1,000. On the strength of it I married my Ella Downey, an Oberlin classmate, also from the Western Reserve. We boarded at Middletown with the family of Alexander Stephenson, appointed at the same time as professor, also from Johns Hopkins. Stephenson and I were supposed to fill the place of Woodrow Wilson, also from Johns Hopkins, who left Wesleyan that year for Princeton. Stephenson had history; I had economics.

Three months before the year was ended President Raymond notified me that I would not be needed the next year, because I was a failure as a teacher. My students were not interested. That certainly should have been shattering news for my Nell, and a baby on the way. But she passed it off as a mistake on the part of the University. Always after, she was the same if I lost a job. She never worried, as far as I could see. Why should I worry?

But I learned three necessities for myself at Wesleyan: short hours of class-work, change in my methods of teaching, and possession of all the facts in planning for the future.

I lectured five hours a week at Wesleyan, and had time for studying to make up my third year at Hopkins, making use of this studying in preparation for my class work. I determined thereafter always to go for short hours of teaching instead of increase in salary; and to use whatever I happened to be investigating as material for my classes, regardless of logical sequence in a course of lectures.

Yet never again was I able to get my hours down to five

per week. I envied European professors who lectured only one hour per week. In Europe the universities started before the common schools, but in America the common schools started before the universities. So, in America, our colleges and universities were built on common school traditions of long hours of class work, and the professor was an upper-grade teacher. But in Europe the professor was an associate of the leisure classes, and education trickled down to the working classes. So I reasoned and took my longer hours philosophically as an American fact. I learned to find time for field investigations during weekends, examination periods, and vacations. When farmers, laborers, or legislators asked me how many hours I taught, and I answered "eight," they said, Well, I suppose the eight-hour day is coming. When I replied eight hours *per week,* they were shocked at my inconsistency in standing for eight hours per day for laborers and only one or two for myself.

The matter came to a public issue when, at Wisconsin, the Legislature and the Governor brought in a famous efficiency expert to investigate the University. He required us to turn in "time-sheets" reporting our hours of teaching. The University faculty appointed a committee, and made me chairman, to protest this factory system applied to the University. We had on the committee a geologist, Professor W. J. Mead, who was a genius in mathematics and tabulation. Our committee changed the time sheets from "hours of work" to "hours of energy," and the legislative committee accepted it. Since then the faculty members make reports each semester on the apportionment of their "energy," regardless of hours, to instruction, research, extension, and administration. So the University joined the movement for "scientific management," but with its version of cost-keeping. I began to trace out the history of the efficiency idea from Ricardo and Karl Marx to Frederick Taylor and the University of Wisconsin.

But, about changing my method of teaching? I never preached at Wesleyan, as I did afterwards at Syracuse about my heterodox opinions; I lectured along in the orthodox authoritative tradition. But I determined, on being dismissed from Wesleyan, that I would spring on my next students all of my inconsistencies, all of my doubts of economic theory, all of my little schemes for curing economic, political, and sociological disease. Perhaps that would interest them. And it did.

Henceforth, for more than forty years, they could see that I was not an authority, did not know much of anything, but was getting ideas from them and incorporating their ideas into mine. I did not quit lecturing, or class quizzing. But my subject-matter was prosperity and depression; unions and unemployment; schemes that I was working on at the time; what the business men, farmers, laborers, politicians, were doing about it; what the economists' theories would lead them to do; what I would do and you would do; and how we would justify it, if we could. Every class meeting or lecture was something unexpected, and they didn't know what was coming next. I was continually changing my mind. All this I learned to do by reason of my blessed dismissal from Wesleyan. It worked. A scholarly classical lady in Madison, after hearing this forty-year story from me at my seventieth anniversary banquet, in my reply to the eulogistic speakers, said to me that my method was Socratic. "Did I know it?" I was surprised. I did not know it. I had read some of Plato's dialogues of Socrates in translation. Socrates was not a university professor looking for a job. He was an interviewer around town. He did not have a marking system on his students. I learned my method by trying to find the easiest way out for myself as an incompetent teacher. At Wisconsin I went further and simply told my students of my experience during the five years after I left Syracuse.

Then, about the possession of facts for forecasting. I understood at Johns Hopkins that their rule permitted a candidate for the doctor's degree to spend two years in residence and one year elsewhere in preparation for his third-year "finals." But I discovered, after I had gone to Wesleyan, that the *last* of the three years must be spent in residence at Baltimore. Well, it was too late. My dream of a Ph.D. degree was given the final bang.

When I got my due notice at Wesleyan I naturally thought of Oberlin and Professor Monroe. Oberlin had a revolutionary history in anti-slavery days, of which she was proud. I myself had written up that history when a student. Professor Monroe knew about my quirks and had nevertheless financed me at Johns Hopkins. Nell and I slipped away before commencement. We were happy. We were coming back to our friendly Oberlin, and I was coming back to Father, Mother, and Sister, after three years of academic venture.

I got an assistant professorship. Nell and I took a little

house on the outskirts. There our baby was born in September. Mother had returned to the old house, across the street from the campus. I scarcely dare to think how she had managed it on the sub-rentals. My brother and I were married the same year, he as a printer in the iron regions of Northern Michigan, I as a teacher in Connecticut. Afterwards we took turns in making a home for Father and Mother. Mother, anyhow, had been cured, at Baltimore, of her rheumatism. Now she could walk and even go on an organizing trip for the Anti-Saloon League as far as Indiana. But my salary, $1,200, would not pay expenses, to say nothing of debts.

I hated to leave Oberlin after only one year, and was ashamed after all they had done for me, but an increase of $800 in salary was too much for me and my wife. Yet the change was not wholly mercenary. We could now support my father and mother in a little house nearby at Bloomington during their last years of life. Then, too, I was getting back to my own Hoosiers. This time they were all Democrats in Southern and Western Indiana. During our three years at Bloomington, my wife broke into print, and got paid for a magazine article long before I did. She wrote on "Mrs. Potter's Inflooence," published in *Munsey's Magazine.* I was proud of it. Never having known the Hoosiers, except me, she saw many things that I had taken for granted as belonging to the Natural Order, which I, years later, in *Institutional Economics,* discovered all economists had done, and I gave to their "natural order" and to mine, the name of Custom. Her story dealt with the most familiar thing I knew in Indiana: the auctioneering of voters to the Republican and Democratic

parties; if auctioneering did not work then the voters who
had sold themselves to the opposite party were made
drunk and were locked up during election day. Indiana, in
those days, was a "pivotal state," and the local parties
could command all the necessary money from their national treasuries. Nell had the characters, vernacular, and
episodes down just as I had known them in my Hoosier
days, but they were news to her. Where I had thought
them great fun and had joined boyfully in them on the
Republican side long before I could vote, she now thought
them corrupt in the views of her imaginary Hoosieress,
"Mrs. Potter." I learned often thereafter that it is not the
men who do the work who can tell the world about it.
They are too familiar with it. It is the investigator from
outside.

We went to Bloomington in 1892. Shortly before,
David Starr Jordan, as its president, had brought Indiana
University to the front by a remarkable faculty of young
men whom he had discovered in the graduate schools of
the New Scientific Method. Our life with these young-
sters and their wives was like getting back to my graduate
days at Hopkins. Jordan was leaving now to do a bigger
thing with more money at Leland Stanford University.
He took with him several of his Indiana faculty, including
my Johns Hopkins friend and fellow student, Professor
E. A. Ross. I was Ross's successor. It was curious that
Ross and I found ourselves again together, a decade and a
half later, this time at Wisconsin. Our reunion was
brought about by our previous Johns Hopkins teacher,
Professor Richard T. Ely, then at the head of the economics department in Wisconsin, after Jordan had fired

Ross from Leland Stanford because his Chinese restrictive immigration views did not suit the California business men and capitalistic farmers.

I found at Bloomington another Johns Hopkins friend, Professor James A. Woodburn, in the history department. Our views were similar, but different enough to be debatable, and they led us together to the meetings with the Populists.

At Bloomington I made my first venture in activities outside the academic field. The American Institute of Christian Sociology was organized, in 1893, to support an American version of what had been known in Europe as Christian Socialism. The aim was to present Christ as the living Master and King and Christian law as the ultimate rule for human society, to be realized on earth. I was made Secretary of the Institute. An eminent minister of the Gospel was made our lecturer. I attended conferences and the largely attended series of lectures at Chicago by our lecturer. I became upset as to the meaning of Christian Socialism and Christian Sociology. On one night of his series our lecturer identified Christianity with pure Anarchism; on the next night he identified it with Communism. He identified each with the love of God. But I now became mystified on the meaning of Love itself. I could not make out whether Christian Socialism meant Love of Man or Love of Woman. On this issue our Institute of Christian Sociology split and disappeared.

I became suspicious of Love as the basis of social reform. I visited the Amana Community of Christian Communists in Iowa. They distinguished rigidly between love of man and love of woman. I studied Mazzini, the great Italian leader of Christian Socialism fifty years before. He founded Christian Socialism on the Duties of Man, including duties to wife and family. Eventually, after many years, in working out my institutional economics, I made Duty and Debt, instead of Liberty and Love, the foundations of institutional economics.

In Bloomington I got myself into trouble and made another mistake. One of my students wrote about me to his relative, Professor W. H. Mace, in the History Department at Syracuse University. A new chair in Sociology had been established there. Chancellor Day wrote to me, in 1895, asking me to come on and see him at a proposed salary of $2,500. I thought it would not hurt to do a little bargaining at Bloomington. I told President Swain, afterwards president at Swarthmore, of the Syracuse offer. Evidently he was loaded, for he immediately pulled the trigger: "Accept the offer at once." I didn't want to accept it and did not want to leave Indiana. But now I had to leave. Never since have I asked for an increase of salary. The exposure is too dangerous. But I have always asked for short hours and provision for a secretary and an assistant. Ultimately I changed my terminology of the classical and hedonic economists' theories of value. Instead of Ricardo's "cost of production," or Menger's psychology of "marginal utility," as the force that determines value, I substituted what, for me, were the more realistic, as well as legally actionable terms, "bargaining power" and "negotional psychology." My mistake was in not knowing that psychology in 1895.

When I went to Syracuse in the spring of 1895, to interview Chancellor Day, I thought I would tell the whole truth. I told him I was a socialist, a single-taxer, a free-silverite, a greenbacker, a municipal-ownerist, a member of the Congregational Church. He answered to the effect: I do not care what you are if you are not an "obnoxious socialist." That settled it. I mistakenly thought I was not of the obnoxious kind.

The Chancellor was a huge commanding figure, about three hundred pounds, an impressive red-faced Methodist minister, latterly almost elected a Methodist bishop, but recently come to Syracuse. One of his trustees, Mr. Huyler, of "Huyler Candy" fame, had established a chair in sociology at the University, and I was to be the first incumbent. I taught ethnology, anthropology, criminology, charity organization, taxation, political economy, municipal government, and other things, all under the name of sociology.

I learned that Mr. Huyler favored municipal ownership. I approached him one time in New York, asking him if he would finance my expenses in making an investigation of municipal ownership in some of the smaller towns of New York State. He willingly approved. I became doubtful of municipal ownership without civil service reform. My results were afterwards published by E. W. Bemis in his book on Municipal Monopolies.

To make the various subjects as interesting for my classes as possible I assigned to each of my students in the taxation class, all of them undergraduates, a city block for which he was to get the "true" values from real estate dealers, compared with the assessed values by politicians. We then presented the results to the city controller who was interested and who had helped us along. To set the criminology class athinking I brought in a half-crazy pauper-tramp, whom I had found somehow, to lecture to the class on his well-remembered but disorderly experiences. I advised the class in advance not to excite him by questions, but to watch me interview him, and afterwards to report to me in writing whether he confirmed Lombroso and the sociologists. He certainly was a success with the class, but for two weeks he kept breaking into the classes of other professors, demanding an opportunity to lecture. I was suppressed by the concerted action of my fellow professors.

I moved my laboratory outside the University. I took the entire class to the local penitentiary, with the consent of the Warden. When I got to the gate I was startled to find that about half the student body was coming along. The next day the Chancellor had a letter from the Warden. The students had been frisking with the prisoners, men and women. I must be disciplined and must make a public apology, which I did. I saw that it was a bad laboratory method in sociology.

I remembered, also from my Indiana days, the short-cut methods of students. We were studying *The Jukes,* by Alexander Johnson, a tribe of intermarried beggars, epileptics, criminals, around Indianapolis. One of my students said there was such a tribe around his home near Bloomington. I organized the class as investigators, with their horses and buggies, to cover a sweep of territory. They brought in family relationships and we built a chart tracing the tribe back to a family named Ham that came across from Kentucky in the early days. But two of the students, in order to get quick results, represented themselves as police authorities. The word spread, and not another Ham would answer any question. A promising contribution to sociology was smothered.

After my Syracuse rebuffs my coöperative investigations were "controlled." I picked out a few students and went with them to the Elmira Reformatory, the Auburn State Prison, the George Junior Republic, the factories. I published, with their help, in 1899, a series of articles in the *American Journal of Sociology* on the "George Junior Republic."

Thus I had tried out several methods of teaching sociology. From the students' standpoint I was a success. When I left Syracuse they presented me with a replica of Hermes and baby Dionysius for my parlor, and a filing case of latest design for my study. At my seventieth anniversary a telegram was read, signed "Thirty-one Syracuse students," saying, "We wish you were here."

I helped the students at Syracuse to start a coöperative store, as I had done at Indiana, on the Rochdale plan. The store room was on the first floor of a downtown office building owned by the University and freed of rent by the trustees. Soon the merchants began complaining of unfair competition. The trustees gradually closed the store. I became skeptical of coöperation in a capitalistic civilization. I continued to lecture on the subject and to visit every coöperative establishment that I came upon in my travels. When I came to Wisconsin, an eminent business man on the Board of Regents had almost persuaded the regents to set up a University store to cut the high cost of living at Madison by selling books and other necessities to students at wholesale prices. The regents asked me for a report on its feasibility. My report said that the merchants of the state would join with the merchants of Madison to bring pressure upon every member of the legislature, and the legislature would cut the University appropriations more than the gain to the students. The project was not started. Afterwards I made "log-rolling" an essential part of collective action and rationing transactions, and defined it according to its several varieties. I have recently noticed that all coöperatives are abolished when Communism, Fascism, or Nazism gets control.

One Sunday morning, at Syracuse, I arrived on the night train from a two-weeks' residence at the University Settlement in New York. In the morning newspaper, on the train, I read an announcement that on that Sunday evening there would be a union meeting of all the churches at the municipal auditorium to protest against the mayor's refusal to enforce the law against Sunday baseball. I was named as one of the speakers. I was startled because I had not received any invitation to speak. The Catholic mayor was my friend, and I was trying to omit modern religion from sociology and stick only to ethnology. I went around immediately to see my friend, the Methodist minister, whose name appeared in the paper as manager of the meeting. I asked him how it came that I was announced as one of the speakers without previous invitation. He said they had been trying to get a workingman to speak but could find only one who was willing. He turned out to believe that the biblical Sunday was Saturday, and that our Sunday came over from the heathen who worshiped the Sun-god. Evidently he was a scholar, but evidently also disqualified as an opponent of Sunday baseball. So they thought I was as near being a working-man as they could find, and announced me because it was too late to ask me by wire.

Chancellor Day was to be the chairman and principal speaker of the mass meeting. There was also the city attorney representing the mayor. His speech was quite political and evasive. I was too timid to speak at the meeting, but finally the minister persuaded me. I looked up one of my labor acquaintances to take me around to all the ball grounds on that Sunday afternoon. We found there large crowds of sober workingmen with their fami-lies, with no admission fees, and with pick-up teams of players from the various industries. At the mass meet-ing of about 3,000 I spoke after the politician. I recited what I had seen during the day. I opposed professional baseball with admission fees on Sunday, but contended that the city should open up free parks, on the abandoned saltpans of the old town of Salina, for all kinds of athletic games for workingmen on that day. As long as employers kept workingmen from having a Saturday half-holiday, the only relief for exercise and sobriety was Sunday. I was hissed by the audience. The Chancellor made no criticism but rather excused me. The daily newspapers stood for me.

A few days afterwards the Chancellor called me to his office. He told me of letters received from ministers and others declaring they would withdraw their children if I were not removed. His reply to them was that I had perfect liberty to speak what I thought, though he would be sorry to lose their children.

A year or so later, in the month of March, 1899, he called me in again. He said that the trustees, at their preceding meeting in December, had voted to discontinue the chair in sociology. I was not dismissed but my chair was pulled out from under me. I did not know about it until three months later. He explained that when he went out on his trips to obtain money for the University from hoped-for contributors, they refused as long as I held a chair in the University. Also, at a recent national meeting of college presidents which he attended, all had agreed that no person with radical tendencies should be appointed to their faculties. Therefore I had no hope for another college position. He was convincing and I never tried to get another teaching job.

I began to draw some inferences from these two Syracuse episodes. It was not religion, it was capitalism, that governed Christian colleges. Afterwards I sought the fundamental reason, and included it in my historical development of Institutional Economics. The older economists based their definitions of wealth on *holding* something useful for one's own use and exchange. I distinguished a double meaning. The other meaning was, *withholding* from others what they need but do not own. This was something real to me and the Chancellor. It made possible a distinction of Wealth from Assets which I began to think economists and laity had failed to distinguish.

When I first drafted, in my early days at Wisconsin, an article on "withholding" as a neglected economic concept, I was dissuaded by an orthodox colleague from publishing it. Eventually, after many years' investigation, I included it in my *Institutional Economics*. I figured that a "chair" in political economy was not physically pulled out from under you, it was economically pulled out by withholding the funds. This was such a customary, legal, and quiet way of doing it, under the institution of private property, that everybody, including economists, took it as a part of the Natural Order not needing investigation. At least, I knew, after 1899 at Syracuse, that holding and withholding were not the same, and that the latter was more important. It was the foundation of assets. It converted Chancellor Day from defiance of Protestants to leg-pulling of Plutocrats.

How easily do assets change people's ideas of God! A few years afterwards, when I was traveling, I met an old single-tax printer whom I had known in Indiana. We worked up a scheme for a national single-tax organization. We visited one of our former single-tax friends. He had meanwhile become a millionaire, on the top floor of a high office building in Indianapolis. We laid before him our scheme requiring funds. He reviewed his own history of becoming a millionaire. He had come to believe that there was an over-ruling divine providence that guided society forward, and nothing we could do would help it forward or hold it back.

I discovered afterwards, at Wisconsin, when I set out to study seriously the history of economic thought, that my capitalist friend's theory of divine beneficence had run from John Locke through Adam Smith to Henry George. God's beneficence meant earthly abundance. My friend was consistent but somehow he had turned the tables on me. Why should we organize a single-tax association to help out God? We dropped our scheme. It was inconsistent with *laissez-faire* and a God of Abundance. I now found the reasons for my obeisance in David Hume and Thomas Malthus. They rejected the theology that God had condemned man to labor on account of sin at the Garden of Eden, which was the theologists' idea of a primitive Golden Age of Abundance. I found that all along I had been following Hume and Malthus instead of Locke, Smith, and George. Malthus had changed the idea of God from abundance to scarcity. So I changed the foundations of economics from abundance, sin, and holding for self, to scarcity, collective action, and withholding from others. It was personal experience for me.

Well, when I brought home the news of the disappearance of my chair at Syracuse, my wife again was not worried, though we had two children and another on the way. I asked the Chancellor to let me off in May with pay, instead of waiting till June. He agreed, and reiterated his forecast of my poor prospects. But my dismissal turned out to be a fortunate happening. It drove me out for five years to live in the struggles of human beings. When the newspaper reporters began bombarding me with questions as to why I was leaving Syracuse, I answered that I had "nothing to say; you must ask the Chancellor." He gave me a rousing send-off. Speaking to a general University convocation, he bewailed the loss of one of their ablest and most popular professors. Then he excited the boys by picturing the donations received for a new ball park, and brought cheers for the new buildings provided by donors to the University. And there was I, sitting on the platform beside him.

So I learned the virtue of silence. It makes eulogists instead of avengers. You keep their secrets. I did not proclaim myself a martyr, like my namesake ancestor. I saw the same virtue of silence often thereafter. Harry Sinclair was sentenced to prison for contempt of court because he refused to testify against his associates. He came out more popular than ever among the capitalists. He kept their secrets. Some fifteen years later, newspapers of Wisconsin were attacking me as an anarchist because I had welcomed Emma Goldman to speak to my classes, and I kept saying to the reporters, "I have nothing to say." My beloved colleague, Professor Steven Gilman, exclaimed to me on the street, "My, John! Your silence makes a loud noise." I explained to Steve. You cannot keep up with the newspapers anyhow. Why try? Make a louder virtue of silence. President Van Hise said nothing to me about it. Likewise, after the War, when I brought W. Z. Foster, later leader of the communists, into my class, President Birge said nothing about it. Van Hise was a geologist, Birge a biologist, accustomed to bringing specimens into their classrooms. Birge thought it was going too far when I introduced Foster to an audience of 2,000 in the University gymnasium. Foster, there, was not a scientific specimen, he was a propagandist.

How different are science and newspapers! When I introduced the labor manager of the Standard Oil Company to a public audience in a University building, a paper of the Progressives denounced the whole University as capitalistic propaganda, and made no reference to the fact that I had recently introduced Foster in a University building. Apparently I had not clearly distinguished science from propaganda. So I made propaganda an essential part of a science of the institutional economics of collective action, which had found no place in the older science of individualistic economics.

IV

FIVE YEARS

ABOUT two weeks after Chancellor Day had informed me of the disappearance of my chair and the bad prospects of finding another, George H. Shibley breezed in on me unannounced from Chicago. I had not been acquainted with him. He had heard me speak on proportional representation at the World's Fair in 1893, where we had organized the Proportional Representation Society. He had been a farm boy in Illinois and had managed the farm, after fourteen years of age, when his father died. He left the farm and became salesman and then general manager for sales for a law encyclopædia. Now, at twenty-eight, after he had acquired a little fortune of $100,000, he retired from salesmanship and wrote, in 1898, a book on *Money*. He advocated bimetallism. Not until twenty-five years afterwards did I realize that he had also proposed to stabilize the movement of wholesale prices by means of controlling the interest and discount rates at the banks. This method occurred to me independently after the War, and I proposed it and discussed it with my classes before I had read the same proposal made by Wicksell, the Swedish economist, in his *Geld und Geldzins,* more than twenty years before, but in the same year with Shibley, 1898.

Afterwards I discovered that the Federal Reserve System was working on the Wicksell theory after 1920, although never acquainted with the economist Wicksell. So strangely do economists anticipate practical men but the practical men discover the economists' theories by experience in great emergencies without knowing anything about the theories. Also my own little ideas were anticipated long before by others without my knowing it.

It was Shibley who, through Senator Owen of Oklahoma, induced the Senate, when the Federal Reserve System was created in 1913, to adopt his own and Wicksell's theory by inserting as one of the provisions of the Act that it should be the duty of the Reserve Board to "stabilize the purchasing power of money." This clause was disapproved by President Wilson, because he did not understand what it meant, and was dropped from the bill in the conference committee of the two houses of Congress, for reasons unknown. After the War, Shibley induced Congressman Strong, from Kansas, to introduce a bill restoring those words to the Federal Reserve Act. On this bill George and I joined.

He was the most generous man I have known. He used up his entire fortune in this pursuit. He offered to divide his income, $5,000, equally with me on a two years' contract, giving to me the same salary as the one I was getting at Syracuse. I was to come with him to Washington or New York and construct an index number of prices to be published weekly. I had to ask him to advance me enough money to get me out of Syracuse. This was to be deducted *pro rata* from my salary during the two years. We decided to go to New York where many of the trade papers were published and where trade association headquarters were to be found. There I could work in the Astor Library, which furnished me a large alcove and liberal assistance.

I found, however, if I was to go around to the trade papers and trade associations to inquire what was the most representative commodity in their industry for which a continuous series could be constructed since 1879, that I needed a statistical assistant for compilation in our office. This assistant George agreed to furnish. I secured, through Professor Richmond Mayo Smith of Columbia University, the help of Mr. N. I. Stone, afterwards labor manager in the Rochester clothing industry and an outstanding efficiency expert. We called ourselves the Bureau of Economic Research and associated with ourselves Professor E. W. Bemis. A refugee like me, Bemis came from Chicago University. He was then creating for himself his own job as expert adviser to municipalities in their contests with privately owned utilities over questions of regulation and public ownership. He financed his end of our Bureau. This was the beginning of my Five Big Years. They furnished me with personal experience stories when I came to Wisconsin in 1904.

It took Stone and me about a year to complete our index series and to get out our first weekly release for the newspapers in July, 1900. This, I learned afterwards from Irving Fisher, was the first weekly index of the general movement of wholesale prices. Some twenty-five years later, Fisher himself, with far more learning than mine, began issuing his weekly index, now published regularly

by leading newspapers. My little index had an untimely
ending.

George had moved to Washington as economic adviser
to the Democratic National Campaign committee in the
campaign for Bryan on the bimetallic issue. He was to
conduct the flotation of our index number as campaign
material. I had voted for Bryan in 1896, and Chancellor
Day had announced in Convocation that there was one
member of his faculty who, he understood, had voted for
Bryan. But he had made no inquiries, and every member
had perfect liberty to vote as he pleased. These creden-
tials had made me *persona grata* with George and the
Democratic Campaign Committee.

Our index number, publication beginning in July, 1900,
showed each week an average fall in prices on the gold
standard, which was quite convincing for George, Bryan,
and the Democrats. But, strangely, beginning about the
middle of August, the index number stopped falling. It
was exactly the same as it had been the previous week.
George wired me that something was wrong, and asked
me to go over the figures again and verify them. This
Stone and I did. The figures were correct. This happened
again the next week. The index number was the same as
the preceding week. Stone and I issued it with anxiety.
George wired again. Then, the first week of September,
1900, that blamed index number, to our consternation,
began to rise. We needed to wait for the lightning only
twenty-four hours. George wired, cancelling my contract,
which had another seven months to run until June, 1901,
but advising me that it was my duty to find other work,
and that he would continue to pay the difference between

my earnings elsewhere and our contract rate. So I know exactly the week when the McKinley Prosperity began, after its slump in the early part of 1900. It was the first week of September, 1900, when I joined the unemployed.

The weekly index number was discontinued. It had to wait twenty-five years for Irving Fisher. I looked up other work and got a few lectures at Cooper Institute. I did not need to call upon George to make up any differences. Within two weeks another wave-length blew in on me. This time it was E. Dana Durand, a former student of mine at Oberlin and then Secretary to the United States Industrial Commission appointed by President McKinley. He afterwards was made Director of the Census and has continued with the Department of Commerce. He asked me to finish for him the report on Immigration which he had begun, at $3,000 salary. I was unemployed and could begin at once. I wished to retain my headquarters in New York, to which he consented, and provided me with assistants and rent for a room in the old Bible House, a few blocks away from the Astor Library.

Thus I had time to philosophize. I had been fired twice within eighteen months, once by the conservatives and once by the radicals, and ended up with a harmless job for the Republican administration. Nevertheless, I voted for Bryan in 1900.

I never could have any hard feelings toward Chancellor Day or George Shibley. My unemployment of two weeks in each case did not last long enough for resentment. Indeed, my condition was improved each time. But I made unemployment the bitterest foe of the capitalist system, whether the big capitalists of Day or the little capitalists of Shibley. George and I remained friends ever after. I admired him. My wife and I took him into our home as a boarder when we moved to Washington in 1901, in order to pay to him the balance of our debt for financing our move from Syracuse to New York. He made our home buoyant, which we needed, for we had just lost our darling Margaret, at four years of age, in New York.

In my office at the Bible House I secured first the assistance of Kate Claghorn, Ph.D. from Yale University. I knew of her outstanding work on Italian immigrants. She afterwards became professor of statistics in the New York School of Social Work. Kate also boarded with us when we moved to Washington, where she also was on the work of the Industrial Commission. Kate and George made for us a scintillating household.

With Kate located in the Bible House I started on a tour of the country. I needed an interpreter who knew economics, and I found him in Abram Bisno, at the Hull House. We traveled together for about six months investigating sweatshops from Chicago to Boston. At Chicago, I took a room around the corner from Hull House, where then and often after I was a temporary "resident." My room near Hull House was a little larger than my bed, and, returning to my childhood ways, I had to take my tub bath in the adjoining room up against a hot stove that helped somewhat to stave off the Chicago winter.

Away from Chicago Bisno and I took rooms in cheap lodging houses or hotels of the immigrant and sweatshop districts. The new model "Mills Hotel" in New York charged us fifteen cents per night, for separate sanitary cubby-holes, within walls and doors raised three to twelve inches above the cement floor for air and scrubbing. It was a relief.

Bisno opened up a new world for me, not only in the life of the immigrant but also in economic theory—Karl Marx and labor unionism. He was my daily seminar for six months. An immigrant, at twelve years of age, with his parents escaping from the pogroms of Kiev, Russia, he had grown up in the American sweatshops of the clothing trade. He had very little schooling and I had him dictate to my stenographer his interviews and interpretations, which I then clipped and pasted into an orderly analysis of the American sweatshop. Was I an editor, or a plagiarist? The chapter was printed as mine by the Industrial Commission "with the assistance of Abram Bisno." The words and thoughts were Bisno's; the credit was mine.

Bisno had worked out a philosophy of his own, through some twenty years of sweatshop life, which I afterwards recognized as Syndicalism and the American I. W. W. He did not want the state, as did Karl Marx, to take over the shops and factories, for he knew the Chicago politicians, but Marx did not. Neither did he want organized labor to take over the sweatshops, for he knew the instability and secret cutthroat competition of his fellow immigrants. He wanted organization of labor that would lay down and enforce the rules to govern the "bosses" in the shops. Yet he could not see how this poorest class of laborers could organize permanent unions. He did not work toward that end. When, in the busy season, the clothing workers could be organized and Bisno could get a job in a sweatshop, he came forward as their leader, and all of them, under his leadership, would get higher piece-rate wages.

Then, as the busy season slowed down and clothing workers were laid off, Bisno was the first to go. He accepted this periodic victimization as the materialistic interpretation of the capitalist system, and so set up a business cycle for himself—in the busy season a clothing worker, in the dull season a real estate agent.

I visited with him in New York one of the garment workers' strikes which occurred at the semi-annual opening of the busy season. It was certainly a mass movement. All of the workers in that branch of clothing were out. Thousands were on an open space in the streets, listening to the eloquence of Emma Goldman, while the organizers of the upstart union were negotiating with their employers. Then Bisno interpreted to me Emma's anarchism. He said that within a month these masses would quit paying dues and would begin secretly cutting wages by connivance with their bosses. The union rules would be evaded and the union would dissolve. So it happened, and I reached a conclusion that the individualistic Jew could not maintain a permanent union.

But I was wrong. I had not distinguished between race psychology and industrial psychology, nor between sweatshop psychology and factory psychology. Ten years later, when the factory system was coming into the garment industry, the Jews organized permanent unions and became the leaders of the other races in that industry. In the sweatshop system of Merchant Capitalism a hundred shops might be working for the same wholesale merchant, each shop of a different race competing against the others. In the factory system, which I named the Employer Capitalism of Karl Marx, they came together. Twenty-five years later I was with Sidney Hillman, a new leader of an enduring union of these same races, from the strikes of 1911. I worked with his aides and seventy Employer Capitalist concerns in setting up their joint scheme of unemployment insurance. The sweatshop boss had become a foreman. The change was the transition from Merchant Capitalism to Employer Capitalism which I had read about in the writings of economic historians. But it had little meaning for me until I saw it operating through twenty-five years in the transition from Bisno to Hillman.

At one of our meetings, in 1924, of the active unionists of the clothing workers at Hull House—"the activity" as they called themselves—Bisno was there, soberly thoughtful with towering forehead and stumbling speech, as I had known him twenty-four years before, but now with gray hairs and wrinkled face. He was treated worshipfully by the younger generation, as might have been a mythical Buddha risen from the past in their midst, although now he was a real estate agent.

After about six months with Bisno studying the immigrants themselves, I took a trip to the headquarters of about half of the national trade unions in order to discover the effects of immigration on unionism. I took along with me, for reading on the train, Webb's new book on *Industrial Democracy* with its remarkable analysis of the "common rule," which afterwards I generalized as the "working rules" of all collective action, including the state. I became acquainted with most of the national leaders of organized labor. I spent considerable time with the bituminous coal mine workers, a huge union of some fifteen races and languages of immigrants, dating from their strike of 1897. While attending, for a week or so, their national "joint conference" of mine workers and their employers, I was struck by the resemblance to the origins of the British Parliament. On one side of the great hall were nearly a thousand delegates from the local unions, an elected representative body. On the other side were about seventy employers appearing directly, without election, as owners of the coal mines. It was evidently an industrial House of Commons and House of Lords, but without a King. I named it "constitutional government in industry," which the editor of the *Review of Reviews* changed to the newspaper title, "A new way of settling labor disputes." When I came afterwards to work with the National Civic Federation, I found they were calling it the "trade agreement," for the promotion of which, without a third party as arbitrator, the Civic Federation had been organized. I dropped much of what I had been arguing for in my book on *Proportional Representation,* as applied to legislatures and Congress; for here was, in actual operation, the main argument of that book, namely the Representation of Conflicting Interests, instead of representation of artificial localities drawn on a map.

The idea went further. It became, after 1911, when I was a member of the Wisconsin Industrial Commission, our model for the administration of Labor Laws by the collective agreements of organized employers and organized labor, with a deputy of the Commission as investigator and conciliator. The essential point, as I learned in 1900 at the miners' joint conference, was the elimination, as far as possible, of a third party, the arbitrator—whether

King, legislature, governor or dictator, handing down
rules and regulations from above—and the substitution of
rules agreed upon collectively, by conciliation. It was to
be, as I then learned in 1900, not Democracy in the historic meaning of a majority overruling the minority, but
representation of organized voluntary but conflicting economic interests.

After thirty years I attempted to work my discovery of
1900 into a system of institutional economics. And now,
after my retirement to my home, and after my book has
gone to press, I am bewildered by the many alphabetical
abbreviations under which the whole nation, through organized conflicting interests and a daring President, is
issuing and revising "codes"—my little "working rules"
from the year 1900. I concede to my radical friends that
my trade-union philosophy always made me conservative.
It is not revolutions and strikes that we want, but collective bargaining on something like an organized equilib-
rium of equality. This I take it, was the social philosophy
of Samuel Gompers. It seems to me the only way to save
us from Communism, Fascism, or Nazism. Yet many of
my employer friends are opposed to it, or seeking to control it. I think they are leading us to Fascism.

This excursion into constitutional government may seem
to have been a diversion from my main work on immigration for the Industrial Commission in 1900. But it was
not. It was a comparison of ten to fifteen races of immigrants from Eastern and Southeastern Europe, where
they knew only dictatorship, in two great American industries to which they had come for what they thought was
liberty. In one of these industries, clothing, they knew,

at that time, only the cycle of revolution and dissolution. In the other, coal mining, they were learning fidelity to contracts—their trade agreements—in forming which they themselves had participated through representative government. It was their first lesson in Americanization, the union of Liberty and Order. Afterwards I wrote a series of articles for the *Chautauqua Magazine* and revised them at Madison for a book on *Races and Immigrants in America,* which was the title of one of my first courses of lectures at the University.

During these trips I contrived another by-product, and laid before Carroll D. Wright, Chief of the United States Department of Labor, an outline for investigation of Restriction and Regulation of Output by organized labor and organized capital. This was not completed until the six-month interval between my service with the Civic Federation and my coming to Wisconsin. It was, in 1904, my initiation into what, in 1934, I listen to over wireless as an amazing nation-wide restriction of output, contradictory to my Adam Smith, Ricardo, Marshall, and the Democratic Party. In thirty years I have seen little acorns grow to mighty trees whirling in a stratosphere of high wind. Whew! Poor me! I am not in it.

When I had finished my report on immigration there was more work to do for the United States Industrial Commission—the writing of the Final Report. Nell and I were eager to go to Washington. Our little Margaret had died while my office was in the Bible House. Nell turned to psychic research and I thought of God as a big cat leading me on to intensity of love for my little girl and then suddenly snatching her away by diphtheria. We buried her in the ancient Eastchester churchyard, with its slab gravestones going back two hundred years, and the bricks of the church brought from Holland. We could not go back to that old house; yet every time I go to New York I walk past it and on to the churchyard.

Owen R. Lovejoy and his wife took us directly from the graveyard to their own home. Lovejoy was our young Congregational minister. Shortly he became, on my eager recommendation, executive secretary to the newly formed National Child Labor Committee, where he did noble work for many years. Albert Shaw, editor of the *Review of Reviews,* said to me when I came back, "The only cure for death is work." So Nell and I must work.

We moved to Washington. There we found the most interesting collection of young economists whom I had known since my Johns Hopkins days. They had been brought in by Dana Durand when he was appointed secretary to the Industrial Commission, after the first reports of their staff of politicians and newspaper reporters had come in and the Commission in consternation had rejected the reports and discharged the reporters. They were the kind of "intellectuals" who come first to the front. More than a year of the Commission's life had been lost in buncombe and futility.

Max West, Durand's expert on taxation, one of the ablest of Professor Seligman's graduates at Columbia University, brought together several of us, with our families, for a communistic settlement in a very big house on the outskirts of Washington, since then covered by a network of railway tracks back of the Union Station. We called it Blithedale. My Nell was made general manager. Durand said it was not communism, it was dictatorship by Mrs. Commons. She certainly worked. The crowd was congenial and brilliant. We kept together until the gradual falling off toward the end of the Commission's term of office. Then Nell and I took a three-story house in a long solid wall of new brick houses on "V" Street, facing the open country, at that time, to the north. There George Shibley and Kate Claghorn were our boarders. We could not tell the houses apart in their solid construction, and often at night I gave a false impression by trying the doors of other houses. Poor Max and his brave wife. He died not long after our life together at Blithedale.

I think the Industrial Commission was the first governmental agency to bring together a staff of trained economists for its work. It was the original "brain trust." The general idea had always been that economists were not practical. But the Commission was temporary. The first permanent branch of government to establish a trained staff of economic investigators was the Federal Reserve Board; the next was the Department of Agriculture, under the second of the three Wallaces, father, son and grandson, all of whom have been cabinet secretaries of that department. At this time the Bureau of Economic Research of the Department of Agriculture was created and headed by my colleague from Madison, Henry C. Taylor. When the second Secretary Wallace died, the Coolidge administration dismissed Harry because he was sympathetic with the uprising of the farmers in the West. But the Bureau continued under Civil Service rules. Now some thirty or more of my former students are at Wash-

ington in several of the organizations of the New Whirlwind.

President Roosevelt must be having quite a time of it,
because I find that some of these students write me to address my recommendations both to the chief of the department in which they are looking for jobs, and to a Democratic politician. I tell the latter that the applicant is a
competent economist and a good Democrat. Since I am
both a University professor and a voter for Bryan and
Franklin Roosevelt, and am besides quite conscientious,
I seem to qualify as a distributor of patronage for brains.
Yet I tell my students to send in their applications as
residents of some state other than Wisconsin. And if they
have now a job that looks permanent, however impecu-
nious, I advise them not to apply. So, from my hill-top
home, I become a kind of employment office for unemployed intellectuals residing in different states of the
Union.

When it came to writing up the Final Report for the
Industrial Commission in 1902, each investigator read his
manuscript to the Commission in committee of the whole;
then took account of corrections, additions, or disagree-
ments of individual commissioners. This became the Commission's rendering of my report on immigration. There
was one commissioner, Hon. T. W. Phillips, member of
Congress from western Pennsylvania, who determined to
write a minority report on the Trusts. He had only two
weeks to do it. He had been the father of the Industrial
Commission law in the Congress. He asked me to write
his dissent for him. I learned now of a split in the ranks

of Capitalism. It was the difference between billionaires and millionaires. Phillips was several times a millionaire, but he might have been a billionaire had it not been for John D. Rockefeller. So I spent two weeks with my little capitalist, a millionaire.

It was a great life. I dined with him every evening at the Shoreham Hotel. He was a bulky, florid individual, some seventy years of age; rather lethargic, but bitter. Our dinner lasted about two or three hours, before I could read to him what I had written during the other fifteen or so. We had two bottles of champagne. You place them in a pail of ice and water on the floor at the right side of the host, while the waiter lifts out a bottle with a napkin and, pointing away from you—pop—the cork is out and the contents bubble up in a stemmed glass before you—Oh! My! Ain't it grand! Never before nor since have I known anything like it. Also we had fifty-cent cigars, moose meat, lobsters and other inspiring delicacies of the rich. I understood that Rockefeller was very abstemious, living on crackers and milk—which was a shame, considering what he might have consumed for the benefit of the poor. But not so with Phillips and me. We furnished employment for thousands, around the wide world. I think that during that period I ate only one meal a day, but took on loads of coffee to counteract the bellyful of high life.

I never could get my attack on the Standard Oil radical enough to suit Phillips. He was always mumbling. So one night I let loose and presented him with something that tore into the very foundations of capitalism. He recovered. My stuff was too stiff. Thereafter I thought I had his measure, and I trimmed my manuscript to fit it. His dissenting report was printed.

Some twelve years afterwards I made a scrappy acquaintance with Rockefeller. On the witness stand of the Industrial Relations Commission, he was thin, solemn, and could not be made by our chairman's drastic questioning to tell very much about anything, because he said he had retired from business twenty-five years before. But we knew he gave the final touch on great questions of policy. Behind the scenes, after the hearing, he was jolly, dancing, with sparkling eyes; gleeful over the many efforts to make him out a criminal. I saw his method of growing a thick skin, and how it happened that he was and still remained a great leader of men, and the richest of men or kings the world had known. To me, Phillips stands for the swollen capitalist of the cartoons; Rockefeller for the Puritan billionaire.

After my two weeks' seminar with Phillips I joined with about the finest and most energetic young man I have known. William English Walling, grandson of William English of Indiana, the millionaire candidate for Vice-President on the Democratic ticket, had been a student with Veblen at Chicago University. He came to me with a timely proposition. The nineteen volumes of the Industrial Commission's hearings could never be read by the people at large. What was needed was a one-volume résumé of the testimony of witnesses. Veblen had himself been constructing this testimony into his brilliant book on modern business organization, published in 1904. Walling was enthusiastic and liberal in expenses. But he had an idea that the best description of the new capitalism would come from those who, like the witnesses, were in the midst of its formation. I was to have charge, with Kate Claghorn, of the office in Washington which Walling rented, giving our attention to boiling down the testimony and reports. Walling made a long trip to the leading men and trade editors of the important industries, including banking. He employed quite a number of them to write up their personal knowledge of the business with which they were connected. When the articles began to come in, Walling sat down to study them. He disappeared for a week or ten days. When he came back, he had thought it all out. He decided to abandon his venture and to pay his staff to release him from his obligations to them. In my case, I had been running toward another of those neurointestinal breakdowns. But Walling most generously sent me to live with my cousin's family at Manassas, Virginia, and to take a walking trip with my eleven-year-old boy down the Shenandoah Valley from Front Royal to the Luray Caverns. Strangely enough, twenty years afterwards, I visited my same boy for a month at the same Front Royal, where he now was farm manager, with the grade of lieutenant, on the five thousand acres of the Remount Station for the Federal Cavalry.

Walling afterwards took a trip to Europe and wrote an excellent book on Russia, besides a significant book on American progressive movements. In his visit to Naples he found a young communist refugee from Russia, who had taken part in the revolution of 1905. He helped Walling on his book. Then Walling sent him to me at Madison, and financed him at the University while he con-

tinued to help Walling in finishing the book, by his trans-
lations from socialist sources in foreign languages. Thus
there came to me, in 1909, my beloved Selig Perlman, at
the age of nineteen, speaking a surprising number of European languages. He helped me for several years on my
history of labor in the United States, and then published
books of his own on the labor movement in this and other
countries through which he had traveled in Europe. He is
devoted to the memory of my wife who admiringly helped
him on his English composition and desperate family affairs. For he had suddenly to bring, by cable draft, his
father, mother and younger brother from the persecution
of the Russian police, who were levying heavy fines on the
families of young Jewish exiles. He is now my brilliant
colleague. From Bisno and Perlman, two exiles from
Russia, I got an insight of the theories and revolutions of
Karl Marx and his followers. Walling became, in later
years, the intimate friend and even the personal agent and
scout of Samuel Gompers, and a staunch supporter of the
organizing efforts of the Negro. Perlman turned from
Marxism to Gompers' Americanized unionism.

When we moved back to New York, in 1902, for my
work with the Civic Federation, we could not go to Mt.
Vernon. We went to the eastern outskirts of Brooklyn.
One of the Tammany capitalists was opening up a tract
of land and had built a sample house in each block. We
bought one of these samples on time payments. When
we left for Wisconsin two years later we sold our equity
for $200. The transportation to my office on Twenty-
second Street and Fourth Avenue required one hour and

fifteen minutes, by elevated to Brooklyn Bridge then street car and several blocks of foot transportation. I was young and energetic. This two hours of transportation was a waste of time. So I wrote on the elevated and surface cars editorials for Hamilton Holt, then editor of *The Independent*. After a few months of this rattling editorial writing I gave it up and read the daily papers like my fellow commuters.

Mr. Ralph M. Easley, secretary of the National Civic Federation, had said to me that, if I wanted a job, to see him. So I went over from Washington to see him. He wished to have me for general work as his assistant. The salary was the same as on the Industrial Commission. I began on taxation, then moved to labor conciliation. Easley had started at Hutchinson, Kansas, in the newspaper business, then moved to Chicago as a reporter and special writer. There he took part in the Civic Federation of Chicago. Lyman J. Gage, former Secretary of the United States Treasury, was its president. It occurred to Easley that what was needed was a national civic federation. He set about organizing it and moved to New York. Such an organization, if it was to be effective, must start off with the most influential and outstanding man in the country. That man was evidently Senator Marcus A. Hanna, millionaire from Cleveland, Ohio, operating in coal mining, shipping, docks, and public utilities. He had collected the funds for nominating and electing President McKinley. I had heard of Hanna frequently in my printing days as a leading capitalist and politician in Cleveland, Ohio. He was popular with the labor organizations. As a coal operator in the Hocking Valley, as early as

1884, he was the first to recognize and deal collectively with the coal miners' union. He was a friend of Daniel Keefe, the notable lumber-shover from the docks of Chicago and then head of the huge longshoremen's union of the Great Lakes. It was through Hanna that Keefe's union was able to organize the dockworkers and sailors over the whole stretch of the Lakes. After the union was disrupted by the United States Steel Corporation, Keefe was made Commissioner of Immigration. I met Senator Hanna only once during my Civic Federation days, and that was when Easley took me over to the Waldorf-Astoria Hotel to report on my investigations of the anthracite coal strike of 1902. Otherwise I reported only to Easley and he deputized me wherever he thought I could fit in. Hanna certainly was the man of financial and political influence who could bring together the great capitalists and the chiefs of the American Federation of Labor. Easley reported to Hanna.

I found in Easley the most illustrious combination that I had known of executive ability, astute insight, critical acumen in holding down to the actual facts, and boyish enthusiasm when we were approaching success in bringing about a settlement of a labor dispute. Our strongest opponents were the National Association of Manufacturers on the one side and the communist and anarchist spokesmen and press on the other. Easley acquired intimate knowledge of all the persons he was dealing with, and their affiliations, before he went ahead on anything. One morning he told me of the saloon I had entered the night before on my way up to a meeting of our X Club of radical intellectuals. It made no difference to him—it was just a piece of information for me. He also gave me inside information of the capitalists, politicians, labor chiefs, with whom he had to do. I never knew whether he employed detectives or not—I think not. His was just a marvellous technique of the long and accurate training of an acute newspaper reporter.

Many of the radical critics of Easley's Civic Federation claimed that it was packed against labor. John Mitchell's national convention of coal miners, at one of their sessions, even compelled him to resign from his membership in the labor group of the Civic Federation on the pain of expulsion from their union. They and those of similar mind figured that the third group representing the so-called "public" in the Civic Federation was anti-labor, as they mainly were, so that the Federation was two-thirds capitalistic and only one-third laboristic. But this was a misapprehension of the organization and purpose of the Civic Federation. It was purely a conciliatory body and did not undertake arbitration. Its purpose was that of bringing about collective bargaining under the new name of "trade agreement," which I first heard from Easley who explained it as an agreement between organized capital and organized labor, without any third party whatever as arbitrator. Its purpose may be recognized in one of the negotiations of a trade agreement that Easley turned over to me. It concerned a threatened street-car strike in San Francisco. The street-car company had engaged strike breakers and had set up a cafeteria and cots in their barns. The strike was to be called by the local union within a few days. By long distance I called William D. Mahon, president of the national union. Easley arranged that Patrick

Calhoun, the head of the financiers and owners, should be
there. The three of us met in my office for two or three
hours. Mahon and Calhoun reached an understanding of
what each would do. Mahon wired his local union to call
off the proposed strike and Calhoun wired the local manager to dismiss the strike breakers and remove the cots, so
that an agreement could be made by the two. A strike in
San Francisco was averted by conciliation and wire from
New York. The Civic Federation was not packed against
labor. For the time being I was the Civic Federation. I
know that I was not packed. I merely pointed out, as the
conversation went along, a few things which each might
do to understand each other and to pacify the local bitter-
ness in San Francisco.

It required a high organization on both sides, so that
one man could speak for each. The union, after many
hasty lost strikes, had amended their constitution to give
to their national president "possession" of the strike, as
they called it. The strike would be "unlawful" and therefore without the aid of the national treasury, if the local
went out without the president's approval. This meant
"possession." It also meant that the national president,
and not the local union, could settle the strike. On the
employers' side the centralization of authority was the
ordinary method of capitalism.

Several other threatened street-car strikes were averted
by me, under Easley's direction, by this long-distance com-
munication with Mahon at Detroit and the capitalists
under Mark Hanna in New York. Easley attended, through
Hanna, to getting the capitalists in the right frame of
mind. It turned out, in every case I think, that, if Mahon

could get "possession" before the local could walk out, Mahon would bring about a settlement. He was a master negotiator. In one case, a New York street-car strike, we were too late. The local hot-heads, led appropriately enough by a man named Pepper, kept "possession." They did not notify Mahon. I got into their last executive meeting. It was my fault in not knowing what was going on. The meeting was the fiery culmination that endorsed a strike the next day. I called up Mahon, but it was too late. He arrived after the walkout. But I admired his masterly way of saving the remnants of the union.

These matters did not work out as well in the steel strike of 1902. The head of that labor organization was a retired minister who had gone into the steel works for a job. The head of the newly combined United States Steel Corporation was the financial House of Morgan. Easley was almost continually on the 'phone, long distance and local. I was assigned detail work. Easley appealed to Gompers and Mitchell, but none of them could reach any understanding with the leader of the union at that time. He, unlike Mahon, Gompers, Mitchell, and other labor leaders whom I came to know intimately through the Civic Federation, had not been a workingman from the start, rising from the lowest positions in local unions and then to the highest position by demonstrated ability of leadership in the negotiations of strikes. He was a previous "intellectual," an unsuccessful or dismissed minister, who entered by a side door, as it were, into the union. He evidently was a capable orator, able to carry off their feet the workingmen whose poor education disqualified them from coping with him in speech making. The Civic Federation

of "capitalists" was anathema to him. Yet, what the
workers really wanted was bread and butter right away,
and a strike to them meant starvation for themselves and
families. But they could not say so effectively, and were
even discarded as enemies in the mass psychology of the
minister's oratory against the abuses of capitalism and
suspicion of the Civic Federation. They started the strike
without funds, or organization, or negotiational leadership, or attempts toward a trade agreement.

It was here that I first learned to distrust the "intellectuals" as leaders in labor movements. I have known scores
of them since then and have found other scores in my long
study of the history of labor movements. Gompers, the
clearest and most outspoken of all trade unionists, denounced them as the "fool friends" of labor. I always
look for them and try to clear them out from all negotiations between capital and labor, and from the councils
of labor. My friends, the economists, often deplored this
antagonism of American labor organizations toward the
intellectuals. But they simply did not know the *kind* of
intellectuals that come to leadership in labor movements.
The kind is not the studious economist and statistician
who cannot make an oratorical public speech, and who
takes a broad social point of view which neither capitalists nor laborers understand. Such an intellectual is discarded and overwhelmed by the passions and cheers for a
speaker who can hold a great audience. I have tried it
and know. Such intellectuals are "class conscious" instead
of "wage conscious," to use the distinction proposed by
my friend Selig Perlman. But the studious economist is
nearly always "social conscious." "Society," however, is a

metaphysical entity which those in the midst of conflict identify with their own class, wage, profit, or rent interests.

Neither did the capitalists play fair with Mark Hanna. This was disclosed years afterwards when the books of the constituent companies were brought to light by Congress. There, in secret, they were bent on destroying ultimately all labor organization. That meant the twelve-hour day. But their open stand in negotiations was quite conciliatory. The Steel Corporation was just then forming and avoiding popular attacks. I learned thereafter to distinguish capitalists from "capitalism," and labor leaders from "labor." The honest, aboveboard capitalist I admire. Many of them I have known. I should like to see them in control of industry. The labor leader who has worked his way up within his organization by trial and error to leadership I admire. I know what lies behind him and can deal with him.

I learned with Easley, as I had previously begun to learn with Shibley and afterwards with La Follette, that the place of the economist was that of adviser to the leaders, if they wanted him, and not that of propagandist to the masses. The leaders alone had the long experience of success and defeat. It was they who took the risks of defeat and deserved the credit of success. The intellectual, a doctor, lawyer, minister, economist, could find a job elsewhere. But the striker must go back to the same employer. If you furnished a worker-leader or a political leader with any material he could use, he alone could tell how much of it he could use, when and how, if it was to "get across" to his followers. Hence I always accepted philosophically what they rejected of my hard work, and stuck to them nevertheless. They were leaders. I was an intellectual.

Easley knew thoroughly this distinction. He dealt only with leaders of organizations, whether laborers, capitalists, or politicians. Afterwards, when it came to working out my theory of Institutional Economics, I based it, not on the assumptions of natural equality of the Declaration of Independence, or of Adam Smith, or of a century of logical economists and their "pure" economics, but on leaders, bosses, and conquerors of the Malthusian more or less stupid and passionate masses. New York City, with its dominance of financial leaders and with its masses of proletariat dominated by Tammany, more or less in collusion with finance, seemed to me wholly un-American. Everybody seemed to depend on inside "tips" and "pulls" with the higher-ups. This did not accord with my Hoosier ideas of liberty. I wanted to go back where the West begins—and did.

I became more deeply involved in the prolonged building trades strike of New York in 1903. There I learned the difference between what I afterwards called the upstart unionism of the newly organized and the stabilized unionism of the skilled trades, the latter named by Hoxie "business unionism." Sam Parks, himself a worker, had organized the Structural Iron Workers in various cities, derived, as they were, from former sailors, common laborers, and the cool-headed dare-devils who risked their lives high up on the newly invented skyscrapers. I could see from my office window the first New York skyscraper, the Flatiron Building on Twenty-third Street, raising its frail skeleton above anything hitherto known in New York. Indeed, the architects had provided for a ten-inch oscillation of the top floor in a high wind. Adam Smith had stated that laborers accepting risky jobs would get higher wages than others, to compensate them for the risk. But he had not figured out how much higher, nor how soon, nor how it would be brought about. The employers, in this case of the structural iron workers, were evidently slow in raising the wages to compensate the risk. Sam Parks did it by strikes, organization and leadership. He was the hero of the structural iron workers. The huge diamond ring which he wore was the gift of his followers, not, as the employers alleged, a bribe from a contractor. They could not understand how it was that the contractors on the Flatiron Building could always pull laborers away from their competitors and could keep on working while other buildings were on strike.

Parks had raised the wages of structural iron workers possibly two or three times as high as they had received in their former occupations. His trade had the strategic position in the new technology. I saw him in action, a thin, tubercular swaggerer, who packed the election meetings of his union, every three months, with his rough riders. He did not realize that the time had come for stabilization, and that this could be brought about through organization of all the contractors of all trades, along with the Flatiron contractors, and an equalization of the competitive level of wages. His vote in the union kept falling off. His opponent was an iron-worker with whom I attended meetings at night. I noticed that always two men were following us. I asked him. He said, "They are my guards." Finally, he won out, the Board of Arbitration was set up, and Parks died of tuberculosis in a Federal prison.

The Board of Arbitration was created with my friend

Samuel B. Donnelly, former president of the International Typographical Union, who had negotiated the agreement with the Mergenthaler Linotype Company, as its executive secretary. Easley had dealt with the employers, I with the unions. I saw daily Easley's thrills in doing something worth while for the joint collaboration of the leaders of capital and labor. Eventually I made activity, and not pleasure or pain, as did the older economists, the focus of my Institutional Economics. Easley was "dynamic" economics.

Many other pieces of work I did under Easley's direction. One of them, the subway workers' strike and collapse, I have written up in my introduction to the third volume of the *History of Labour in the United States*. In another case a big capitalist had a strike on his hands in the West, and wanted me to approach the national president of the union to call it off. "There is a thousand dollars in it for him," he said, "if he is that kind of a man." I reported to Easley. I knew personally the national president. Should I approach him? Easley instructed me to inform the capitalist by 'phone that the labor leader "was not that kind of a man." I spent five months with John Mitchell at his modest hotel in New York during the anthracite coal strike, also described in the third volume of the *Labour History*. I agreed with a prominent lawyer who said to me that "Mitchell made the coal operators look like thirty cents." With Walter E. Weyl I made a two weeks' investigation of the strike throughout the anthracite field, reporting to Easley on the probable duration of the strike. I made a trip as far west as Wisconsin, helping Easley organize his department on taxation. This department was dropped after the organization of the National Association of Tax Commissioners, whose first meeting I attended.

I hated to leave Easley, but Professor Ely had worked up a position for me at the University of Wisconsin. He had consulted Easley. I asked Easley to let me off at the end of 1903, to finish my work for the Department of Labor in the six months before moving to Wisconsin. As said above, I had submitted to Colonel Wright an outline of investigation of Restriction and Regulation of Output by Capital and Labor. At that time I expected to do the work myself, for $1,600. But some time afterwards Colonel Wright met Charles M. Schwab who was much interested in having that work done. Wright then offered to place four men of his staff under my direction. I asked that one of them should be Ethelbert Stewart. He asked how I happened to ask for Stewart. I answered that I had never met him but had seen an able article by him in one of the bulletins of the Department. So, when I went to work in New York with the Civic Federation, the four men reported to me. When Ethelbert Stewart came in, he was a great mad lion with shaggy mane. I could see that he was sore at being placed under the academic direction of a college professor. I found that, back in the 'eighties, he had been a leader among the Knights of Labor, and editor of their important paper in the mining regions of Illinois. I relieved his inward rage against reporting to me by sending him off to Illinois to write up an investigation, all his own, on the rules and regulations of the bituminous coal miners' union in that state, where they were the most powerful of all the state branches of the union. Stewart's investigation lasted for more than a year. He turned in what I think was the first American detailed investigation of labor unionism, a notable piece of work. I asked him to come to Brooklyn during the six months of my final preparation, to help me edit his and the other contributions and to make the generalizations after each contribution that would unite the whole into a unified volume. It was published as a special report by the Department of Labor.

It was during those discussions with Stewart that I first began to develop the "academic" general principles underlying unionism and collective bargaining, which ultimately formed a major theme of my *Institutional Economics*. What started out, with Colonel Wright, as a restriction of output became a detail in the larger social problem of the working rules of all collective action in control of individual action. I think this was the first time in the Department of Labor, except for his short article which I had read, that Stewart was permitted to get full credit for an independent piece of investigation. I could see, from observing the other three men assigned to me, how it was that Colonel Wright developed the military organization of privates carrying out the detailed orders of their commander. They were remarkably accurate in copying figures and making calculations, the accuracy of which was something that Wright strongly insisted upon. But they had no insight or understanding of what it was all about. Even the special volume which we prepared is catalogued in all the libraries under the name of Carroll D. Wright. I could thus see in my own case how repressive on individual initiative is the military regimen of giving the credit to a commanding officer. Stewart eventually rose to be the Commissioner of Labor Statistics, when the Department of Labor had been raised to a political cabinet position. He retained that position for some time, even after the usual retiring age. Yet he always distrusted the academic mind, including my own.

The two other pieces of independent investigation were made for the volume on output—one by Walter E. Weyl on the anthracite coal industry and one by Professor John H. Gray on the British unions. These required no editing. I wrote up the typographical union. That investigation included my first acquaintance with German printers and a German newspaper publisher and editor. The editor took me up to the linotype room and loudly "bawled out" the whole array of linotype men. But there they sat without a word. They certainly had the publisher tied up, turning out only about one-third as much work as in the English offices. But I noticed that nearly all of them were gray-haired. I never knew so many gray-heads in a printing office. I tried to make a census of their ages compared with the ages of printers in non-union, typographical union and the government printing office. But as soon as I touched on ages they shut up and nothing more could I get. It was evident to me that their "closed shop" was their system of old-age pensions. I got my first glimpse of German industrial psychology, the psychology of force rather than negotiation, and I have more or less followed it through until I see it end in Nazism, with the annihilation by force of all kinds of labor unionism.

SELF, 42, 1904

V

WISCONSIN

I WAS born again when I entered Wisconsin, after five years of incubation. I came at the time of the University Commencement, in 1904, and heard the new President, Charles R. Van Hise, risen from the Geology Department, tell the faculty, in his inaugural address, that each teacher was expected to get proportionate credit for Instruction, Research, and Extension.

Now, in thirty years, I see it accomplished. During my semi-retirement, my former and present generations of students come vividly before me; I review my Friday Niters; I recount my pieces of research and administration; I listen to "WHA, the Wisconsin state-owned station," which broadcasts "The College of the Air." I hear the University, or the State Departments, talking to the boys and girls on the free instruction open to them from childhood to the post-graduate and professional degrees; telling all the people of our citizenship, our highways, our forests, our three thousand lakes, our unemployment, mortgages and prices. There is Jennie Turner, now with a State Department—she is for me Jennie McMullin, my Irish girl of years ago—telling them of vocational education, of the State Library that will loan books to study classes, without charge; telling them of beautifying their homes and roads. There are the University professors telling them of electricity, chemistry, the social sciences, music, and other researches and teachings of the University. It is President Van Hise's instruction, research, extension.

I came too, in 1904, at the time of another commencement held in the same University building. It was the last Republican State Convention preceding the new system of primary elections. It gave to Robert M. La Follette, after two terms as governor, control of both branches of the legislature. The socialists of the factory system of Milwaukee and the shore of Lake Michigan had been organized in 1898, led by Victor Berger, from Austria. The small farmers and the younger generation of professional and business men had been organizing since 1894, led by La Follette. His French family came from across the Appalachian Mountains, but he came from a small farm where they settled in Wisconsin. The big business and the financiers from New York, who previously had dominated the Republican Conventions, were led by Emanuel Philipp, afterwards governor of the state during the World War. His family came from an Italian Canton of Switzerland, but he, like La Follette, came from a small farm in Wisconsin. I saw, from the platform, these two alignments split the Republican party. The next day the followers of Philipp held their own convention. The Democrats were a split minority and lined up with the Republican split, except for a skeleton organization of professionals, during the forty years 1894 to 1934. The three groups were Progressives, Conservatives and Socialists, each with representatives in the state legislature. The issues were no longer political—they were economic. I made, during these thirty years, Conflict of Interests, not the Harmony of Interests of the classical and hedonistic economists, the starting point of *Institutional Economics*.

My new birth, in 1904, thrust me into this conflict. Wisconsin, with two and a half million people, has been a miniature for me of one and a half billion people around the world, driving on to Communism, Fascism, Nazism. The State University and the State Government, only a mile apart in a small city, have been a focus, unique among the states, for instruction, research, extension, economics, class conflict, and politics.

I had met La Follette as governor in 1902, on my taxation trip for the National Civic Federation. He was then bringing to Wisconsin the new system of *ad valorem* taxation which originated in my own Indiana when I was there some seven years before. This system based the taxation of railways and other public utility corporations, not on the older ideas of corporeal property located in the state, but on the newer idea of the state's share in the total value of the "intangible property" of the corporation as a unit throughout the United States, evidenced partly by the sale-value of its securities on the New York stock market. I had known the editor of the *Indianapolis News,* who drafted the Indiana law. He had explained to me, in 1895, the principle of the new system of taxation, afterwards sustained by the United States Supreme Court in a case coming up from Ohio. I had not then seen its significance. But now, seeing the intense political conflict in Wisconsin over this same economic issue, I got my first idea of a "going concern" existing wherever it does business, distinguished from a "corporation" existing only in

the state of its incorporation. In the course of the next
thirty years I worked out the idea of going concerns as
existing in their transactions of conflict, interdependence
and order.

La Follette had been a member of Congress from the
Madison district, as early as 1884, serving on the Ways
and Means Committee under its chairman, William Mc-
Kinley. There he had won approval of the Republicans
by his speeches supporting, with new arguments, the tariff
and the tax on oleomargarine. But in 1894 he resented the
control of the Party in Wisconsin by the financiers, and
started on his ten-year campaign to wrest that control
from them. Afterwards, middle-aged men, now opposed
to La Follette, have told me of the inspiring effect La
Follette had on them in this ten-year campaign when they
were younger. He opened up to them a noble idea of
patriotism for the state, wherein there should be no cor-
ruption in politics, no control of governors and legislatures by the lobbyists of corporations, no "machine" politics controlling the party conventions. Instead there would
be a resurrection of the early American idealism of government by the people themselves.

I began to learn from this a new "economic" interpretation of history and class struggle to take the place of
the Marxian "materialistic" interpretation. As long as La
Follette's inspiring patriotism was working along the lines
desired by an economic class, they supported him. But
after he had written into legislation what they wanted
they deserted him and went over to the conservatives.
First, small business men and much of the great lumber
interest of the state supported him in his attack on the

railway corporations to obtain equality of taxation and control of rates which interested them as shippers. When these objects were attained they went over to the opposition. La Follette relied upon them at first. By far the wealthiest lumber man of the state, Isaac Stephenson, bought a daily paper in Milwaukee in order to have at least one metropolitan daily for the extension of the new ideas of taxation and freight-rate control. La Follette stood loyally by him, and succeeded, in the legislature of 1907, in overcoming opposition among his own followers and electing Stephenson to the United States Senate. Afterwards he said to me, in the Senate lunch room at Washington as Stephenson was passing by, "They are getting him."

La Follette was stigmatized by his opponents as a "boss." But I could never see it that way. I had known, at close contact, the Tammany boss system in New York. I began to analyze the difference between a boss and a leader. The boss controlled the jobs—the means of livelihood of his followers—through a hierarchy of district bosses down to the rank and file of the voters. The "boss" could not himself be elected to a public office. He was merely the head man in a private association of these actual and would-be bosses. By this economic control of subordinates he named and elected the public officials and obtained funds from the financiers who wanted franchises or other special privileges. La Follette had shown by his organizing ability and the most determined will-power that I have known, that he had all of the qualifications needed by a boss. But, at the high point of his success in gaining control, in 1904, of the convention and the Republican organization—also a private association—he delib-

erately deprived himself of the instruments of bossism.
He had induced the people to approve direct primary
nominations of public officials, thus doing away with the
convention system.

Afterwards I saw how it worked. To the legislature
came a Democratic single-taxer for whom I drafted a bill
on that subject, Edward Nordman, a pioneer farmer from
the North Woods, not endorsed by any political party.
His campaigns were merely postal-card campaigns, stating
his single-tax principles directly to the individual voters of
his county.

I saw again how it worked against La Follette himself.
Irvine L. Lenroot, of Swedish descent, was his leading
lieutenant, chairman of the convention in 1904, and
Speaker of the Assembly in the notable sessions of 1903
and 1905. In the preceding campaign of 1904 La Follette,
through his control of the convention, had nominated and
elected a Scandinavian immigrant, James Davidson, as
lieutenant governor on the same ticket with himself as
governor. Here La Follette was admittedly a boss. But
Davidson, when he became governor, after La Follette resigned to go to the United States Senate, turned out to be
a conservative, lining up with that wing of the party. La
Follette determined to have Lenroot nominated in the
primaries of 1906 against Davidson, the conservative
candidate. He made a marvellous campaign, with large
and enthusiastic audiences, through the state, in favor of
Lenroot. When he made his last speech, on the night before the primaries in the University gymnasium, to a
crowded enthusiastic audience, he was beaming with
excitement. He said to me on the platform that, judging

by his meetings, Lenroot would be nominated by 50,000 majority. But the next day Lenroot was defeated by a large majority. La Follette had mistaken enthusiasm for himself for enthusiasm for Lenroot.

So there was driven home to me the difference between a leader and a boss. After studying the decisions of courts on economic disputes, I made the difference rest on the legal-economic distinction between persuasion and coercion. The boss controls by economic coercion, the leader controls by persuasion. La Follette had nominated Davidson, and was a boss. La Follette by persuasion could not nominate Lenroot against Davidson, and was merely a leader. The people of Wisconsin, under his leadership, would no longer stand for bossism, but they were eager for leadership. La Follette, at his climax of political power, had reduced himself from boss to leader.

Another demonstration of his abdication from bossism had come even more vividly to me in my first six months at Madison. La Follette had not, as far as I know, made a single reference, in his campaign of 1904, to civil service reform. After the November election, when he was undisputed boss, he asked me to draft the best civil service law to be derived from a study of all similar laws in the country. He made only one stipulation. All existing employees of the state, except the heads of departments and elected officials, were to take the same civil service examinations as others, to determine whether they were competent to carry on efficiently the work for which they had been appointed. This included his own appointees during his preceding governorship of four years. I mildly explained that it had never been done. Always the distinguished

civil service reformers, like Grover Cleveland, had
"blanketed in" the existing appointees. La Follette's plan
was a desertion from his own followers who got public
service jobs by working for him. He did not argue with
me. He simply replied that was the way he wanted it.
He abdicated bossism.

It was charged in the state that this provision of the
act was mere bluff. La Follette's own appointees would
not be removed for inefficiency by a Commission appointed
by himself. I never followed it up to see what happened.
I only know that he asked me to become one of his first
board of three commissioners. I had come from another
state and had not "worked" for him. I could not accept,
and he appointed a professor from the Department of
Political Science.

A curious outcome, for me, of his civil service law,
occurred six years later, when I was promoting before legislative committees the adoption of the Industrial Commission law which my students and I had drafted with the
approval of the Progressive leaders. I found myself in
direct opposition to the civil service law which I had
drafted six years before. A clause in the proposed law
exempted from civil service examination the "deputies"
of the Industrial Commission. But La Follette's principles
had percolated through his followers, and in the legislature they exclaimed that they wanted no "pets" in this
new Commission. They struck out the exemption.

After I was appointed to that Commission for the short
term of two years by Governor Francis E. McGovern, my
colleagues and I—Charles Crownhart, previously chairman
of the Republican State Committee and afterwards Justice

on the Supreme Court of the state; and Joseph E. Beck, previously Commissioner of Labor and afterwards member of Congress and then member of the State Agricultural and Market Commission—visited the State Civil Service Commission. We explained to them what we needed in the qualifications of our deputies. We needed especially the qualification of mediators and conciliators between the conflicting employers and employees of the state, as well as deputies capable of taking testimony and making investigations that would stand the scrutiny of the courts. We proposed that the civil service examinations should be "elimination contests," but that the actual appointments for the positions should be made on oral examinations and recommendations by the advisory committee of organized employers and organized labor which were authorized by the new law and which we had already begun to set up. This proposal was not contradictory to any of the civil service laws as I had studied them. The Civil Service Commission accepted the proposal, with certain safeguards. Several satisfactory deputies were appointed to these responsible positions. The employers' representatives even selected two socialists, William M. Leiserson and Fred H. King, to have charge of the Milwaukee State Employment office, and a trade unionist, Stewart Scrimshaw, to administer the new apprenticeship law.

I was glad that I had been defeated by the devotion to civil service rules which La Follette had succeeded in bringing home to his followers. It relieved us of all political pressure from Progressives for jobs and gained for the Commission the confidence of employers to whom we were supposed to be antagonistic. It was this new kind of civil service, having the confidence of capital and labor, that made possible, twenty years afterwards, the enactment of an unemployment insurance law entrusted to the Industrial Commission for its administration through a similar advisory committee of organized employers and organized employees. We had discovered in 1911 what La Follette had known in 1904, that progressive legislation could not be made enduring and constitutional before the courts—and, in our case, conciliatory toward organized employers and employees—except by a civil service law in which the Progressives, like their great leader, denied themselves political preference for jobs.

A stunning illustration came to us in the Milwaukee employment office. The Industrial Commission law had given power to the commission to remove existing officials and to appoint others in their places. We removed the head of the Milwaukee office, a political appointee, and, as stated above, named two socialists in his place on the recommendation of our advisory committee of employers and trade unionists. Shortly after, the Progressive governor of the state, who had appointed us, came to us with the alarm that a delegation of eminent citizens, including a judge of a Milwaukee court, had protested to him against this amazing concession to what they argued was the hot-bed of socialism in Milwaukee. Our chairman, Mr. Crownhart, proposed a solution. Let the governor invite his delegation of political supporters to meet in Milwaukee with the employer members of our advisory committee who had joined in recommending to us the appointments. The meeting was held. We learned afterwards of the drubbing which the employers gave to their political fellow citizens. The political incumbent, they said, had been running merely a loafing place for "heelers," and the employers could not take on anybody sent to them for jobs. Indeed, they had been forced to set up a private "citizens'" employment office, alongside the state office, in order to find jobs for the competent unemployed. These two socialists were already operating that office and sending to the employers the kind of applicants they needed in their shops. The socialists and trade unionists thus appointed had been graduate students of mine, and naturally neither I nor my colleagues on the Commission took any part in the conferences or oral examinations. We were simply able to point out, to anybody who objected, that the parties most directly concerned—organized capital and organized labor—had really made the appointments and would appoint their successors.

As I look back over my thirty years in Wisconsin and recall the many attempts, including my own in 1911, to emasculate the civil service law, I conclude that the greatest service La Follette rendered to the people of the state was that civil service law of 1905. Without that law, and the protection which it gave to him and succeeding governors in making appointments, his own administrative commissions on taxation and railway regulation would soon have broken down. The state, in thirty years, has switched from Progressives to Conservatives and back to Progressives and then to Democrats, and these shifts have always brought open or covert attacks on the civil service law. Without the civil service law, none of the later so-called "progressive" laws involving investigation and administration could have been enacted. Their enactment depended on confidence, on the part of the strenuously conflicting economic interests, in the public officials to whom the administration of the laws should be entrusted.

I sometimes have heard from people of other states that the Wisconsin pioneer success in administering progressive legislation must have come from the large German element in the state who brought with them the traditions of the efficient government of Germany. But the Germans in Wisconsin, although exceeding in numbers any other of its many nationalities, have been the least active, politically, of all. The civil service law was sprung on the state by one man, La Follette.

I now see that all of my devices and recommendations for legislation in the state or nation have turned on this assumption of a non-partisan administration by specially qualified appointees. When I made my report for the Industrial Relations Commission in 1915, the report was attacked, in and out of the Commission, on the ground of "bureaucracy" and government of the lives of the people by "experts" instead of government by "the people" themselves. Germany was pointed to. It was said that I wanted to create political jobs for "intellectuals" like myself. Now that the Democratic politicians, after thirty years of taking their hopeless chances in getting a preference in Wisconsin, by nullifying the civil service examinations, on account of their work for the party, have openly avowed the tradition from Andrew Jackson and William Jennings Bryan, that a good Democrat is as good as or better than anybody who passes a civil service examination, I give up, after seventy years of age, and wonder whether I have been wrong all along. Although a good Democrat myself I am glad that I am retired and can sit at my window cogitating about my philosophy of scarcity and conflict. Through it all, I go back to La Follette's instruction to me in 1905, and to my later conclusions when I made Administration more important than Legislation. Legislation furnished the authorizations. Administration was legislation in action.

In my civil service bill-drafting of 1905 I made another discovery. It was Charles McCarthy. In his particular field he was as distinct a personality and pioneer as were La Follette and Berger in the political field. His versatility, ingenuity, determined will-power and sympathy for the underdog typified to me the Irishman the world over. He had begun among the shoe-workers in Brockton, Massachusetts, and then had worked his way through Brown University and the University of Wisconsin. I came to depend on him for everything I tried to do in the state of Wisconsin. He seemed to know everybody in the legislature and in the local politics of the state, and knew just who were leaders and how they would react. When, in his last sickness, broken down by zeal, he was leaving for Arizona, I visited him I could think of only one thing to do—give him my picture. In his weakness and lonesomeness he cried with love for me. He knew he would never come back alive. When he did come in his coffin his body rested in state at the capitol, and the legislature voted a bronze tablet in the Assembly Hall where his strong profile with his Hapsburg jaw remains as his monument.

McCarthy made one mistake. He was induced, in 1918,

to become a candidate for United States Senator as a Democrat in the primary elections. He received only 14,000 votes. He was not a vote-getter—he was a legislator. He brought to Wisconsin the first state-wide vocational and continuation school legislation in the country, after a thorough study of the subject in Europe. More than any one else he was responsible for the perfected coöperative legislation of the state. His famous Irish colleague, Sir Horace Plunkett, the founder of coöperation in Ireland, came to Wisconsin to help McCarthy in that legislation. He afterwards wrote an article, in *The Nineteenth Century* magazine, on "McCarthy of Wisconsin; the Career of an Irishman Abroad as it appears and appeals to an Irishman at Home."

I had met McCarthy two years before, on my taxation trip to Madison. He took me up to the attic of the state capitol, to see his "clipping bureau." He certainly "buttonholed" me. His clipping bureau was to be an aid to members of the legislature in drafting their bills. He was appointed to the position by the Wisconsin Free Library Commission, mainly an ex-officio body. This made his position practically a permanent civil service appointment, independent of party politics. Afterwards when he was investigated by the legislature and the attempt was made to remove him during the administration of Governor Philipp, this peculiar civil service appointment made him immune from political attacks.

In 1902 I could not take in all that McCarthy's clipping bureau implied. But, in 1905, in drafting the civil service bill, I found that here was an entirely new kind of library. It was telegraphic. McCarthy wired to civil service organizations, to state governments, to individuals, for statutes, bills before legislatures, clippings, and comments. Within a day or two after La Follette requested my help on the bill, McCarthy had me supplied with everything one could need in drafting that bill. I soon could submit to him and to La Follette a preliminary draft. I never before had known such a quick-action library. I learned to send my students to his library, often to do most of their work there in preparing their topics and theses. They assisted in the investigations as aides to the bill drafters. McCarthy had, or would get immediately, almost everything one might need on all sides of every debatable issue before the public, or the legislature, or Congress. When the new capitol was built, after the fire of 1904, McCarthy's Legislative Reference Library had one of the four wings on the same floor with the Senate, the Assembly, and the Supreme Court. The regular State Law Library was on the floor above. McCarthy even furnished me with an office when I was working with legislative committees. Most of all, his stubborn criticism of every detail in my work, his participation in our conferences, and his fertile suggestions forced me to the most careful self-criticism that I had ever known except during my apprenticeship under Easley.

No wonder that this library came to be stigmatized as the "bill factory." I figured out the reasons. Prior to McCarthy's coming, the legislators could look only to the lobbyist lawyers to help them draft their bills. Now McCarthy furnished them with both investigators and lawyers paid by the State. If a farmer legislator wished to amend the fish and game laws, he made a memorandum of what he wanted. This was kept on file by McCarthy in self-protection, and McCarthy's staff presented to the legislator the bill ready for introduction. It was a "bill factory," indeed, but operated by the state instead of by private lobbyists.

So it was when magazine writers wrote articles on "a university governs a state." I could never see it that way. I was never called in except by Progressives, and only when they wanted me. I never initiated anything. I came only on request of legislators, of executives, or committees of the legislature. The same was true of many other members of the faculty. A university is not a government, it is a collection of individuals. It has as many differences of opinion as do the people at large. Each professor is independent of all the others. He can furnish only technical details and then only when he is wanted by politicians who really govern the state. So with the "brain trust" at Washington. I see individuals coming and going according to whether or not they furnish the President with what he wants. A different President has a different brain trust. The faculty of the University of Wisconsin has always been perhaps nine-tenths on the conservative or reactionary side. Magazine writers, coming to write up Wisconsin, have been surprised to discover this fact. They expected to find a radical university. I even had to point this out to a conservative employer writing to me from Milwaukee. He had an idea that the University was socialistic, or at least that it always promoted the "labor" side against the "capitalist's" side. He wanted the "employers'" side represented on the faculty. When I replied that the University had a great majority of its faculty in several colleges—engineering, law, commerce, the college of liberal arts, the economics department—mainly devoted to training students to serve the interests of business and employers, he verified my statement and so advised me.

I saw again, in 1907, how McCarthy's "bill factory" worked. Senator La Follette and Speaker Herman L. Ekern, of the Assembly, asked me to aid the committees of the legislature in drafting a law that would extend to municipal and interurban public utilities the regulation already exercised over railways through the act of 1905. McCarthy gave me a room in his library, and during the five or six months' session of the legislature I met there the representatives of the public utility corporations and worked with Mr. M. S. Dudgeon, of McCarthy's legal staff, in drafting the bill. My qualifications, I presume, were that I had recently returned from a joint investigation under the National Civic Federation of some thirty-five municipally and privately owned gas, electric, light, power, and street-railway utilities in England and America. This investigation was then in course of publication, in three volumes, by the National Civic Federation. It was, for me, the most illuminating, but ended as the most terrifying experience I have had.

The investigation grew immediately out of the change, in Philadelphia, from municipal ownership to private ownership of the gas works. The politically managed municipal works had been the most disastrous failure of its kind in the country. It was a huge inescapable argument against the advocates of public ownership on the issue then creating the most excitement throughout the country. The newspapers gave almost daily reports of the progress of our joint investigating committee. So confident were the private owners in Philadelphia of the remarkable contrast between the two systems in that city, and so much concerned were the leading advocates of public ownership, that it was possible for Mr. Easley, of the National Civic Federation, to raise a large sum of money to finance the investigation.

The general commission, sponsoring the investigation, had a membership of one hundred and fifty widely known publicists, corporation chiefs, and leaders of labor. Its executive committee of twenty-four included such names as that of its chairman, Melville E. Ingalls, chairman of the Board of Directors of the Big Four Railroad, who also was chairman of the investigating committee; John Mitchell of the Mine Workers; Isaac N. Seligman, of the financial house of J. and W. Seligman and Company, treasurer; Louis D. Brandeis; Samuel Insull; Carroll D. Wright; and others at that time equally well known.

The Committee on Investigation, with twenty-one members and Mr. Ingalls as chairman, was so appointed that the "technical reports" on all points of dispute should be made by one expert nominated by the "pros" and one nominated by the "antis," "these two to work side by side and prepare a joint report." In a few instances, especially on the financial, engineering and historical aspects, a single expert was appointed where the "pros" and "antis" could agree on the nominee. In my own field of "labor and politics" my working colleague was my old friend of the typographical union and the single-tax persuasion, Mr. J. W. Sullivan. Mr. Sullivan was appointed as an "anti" and I as a "pro." He had been associated with Henry George in the New York campaign twenty years before, and was a close friend of Samuel Gompers, whom he afterwards represented on the War Labor Board. My visits with him to the British cities, the cathedrals and the ancient landmarks, were extremely interesting and were a new experience. This was my first trip, but Sullivan had made many trips and was an all-round scholar, speaking several languages. His social philosophy went far over toward the *laissez-faire,* free trade, even the anarchism or at least semi-syndicalism of private organizations of capital and labor unions.

The fifteen members of the investigating commission, who spent some five months in England, were so luxuriously entertained that it might have been thought we were on an old-fashioned American junketing party. But I discovered that it was only the British "week-end," or "four-o'clock tea," or noon-day banquet, descended from the aristocracy of Britain, and taken over by capitalists. No investigating, according to my ideas of investigation, could be made during those hours. I remember when we went to a noon-day reception given by the Lord Mayor of London, we had to rent Prince Albert coats and silk top hats. As we processioned along the street, after leaving our carriages, I could think only of American minstrel performers parading the streets in advertisement of their coming show. My fellow investigators were very solemn and unresponsive when I suggested to them this parallel. It was a serious matter to banquet with the Lord Mayor, decked in his gold insignia of office, and eating from golden plates along his banquet table served by purpled waiters in knee breeches. Mr. Ingalls had previously warned me against my golf cap which I had been wearing around the seats of the mighty in England. My labor colleagues on the Commission were evidently subdued by their new dignity. But they were ready to explode if we could get off by ourselves. At a reception given to our delegation by the Duchess of Sutherland, in London, we marched across the broad floor of her four-story lobby to where she stood on a landing leading up to the velvet stairway. I was so oppressed by the solemnity and speechlessness of our delegation that when I shook hands with the Duchess, surmounted as she was, by her diamond tiara, while the decadent-looking Duke stood at one side with his blue silk ribbon diagonally across his big shirt front, that I exclaimed to the Duchess that we were Americans coming over here to study socialism. She replied, "Well, this is the place to come," and I passed on. The others said nothing, but solemnly bowed and grabbed her hand. As soon as we reached a sitting place in the Duke's amazing picture gallery, McNulty, president of our American national union of electrical workers, burst out, "You needn't brag—the *Duke* spoke to me." We all asked eagerly what did the Duke say. "Stand aside, young man." That was what the Duke said to McNulty. When our delegation jointly interviewed Sir George Livesey, head of the huge gas company in London, he added as his attraction to an invitation for a reception to us that he would "try to have a Lord there." We were entertained at a garden party by a wealthy merchant trading to India, in his high-walled estate in London, and at another given to us by Sidney and Beatrice Webb outside London.

I kept wondering, all along, how it was that British capitalists, spending so much time in copying the idle aristocracy, could have created the greatest economic empire known to history. I thought of the abstemious Puritans who were the founders of British capitalism. I thought of my Adam Smith who pictured the hard-working and "parsimonious" manufacturers and merchants as those who created the "wealth of nations" by saving and working, in contrast to the spendthrift aristocracy who lived on their "monopoly" of land and "reaped where they did not sow." It seemed to me, here, in our brief acquaintance with capitalist leaders, that we must surely be looking upon the decadence of British Capitalism. I noticed afterwards that younger British economists wrote of it as such. I felt more satisfied and more at home when I could go around with the labor leaders and visit the homes of the working people. Even John Burns seemed to me remote from the life of the working people. I had known about him as the leader of the London dock workers in 1889. Now, as the first labor member of a British Cabinet, he introduced me around to members of Parliament on the tea-drinking terrace of Parliament House on the bank of the Thames. I hunted up Appleton, head of the General Federation of Trade Unions, an organization separating itself from the political Trades Union Congress and from its Parliamentary Committee which was just then becoming the Labor Party. I attended, with Appleton, at Southampton, the meeting of his Federation. I was called on for a speech. I could not enter into the political and trade-union divisions in the British Labor movement. I could think only of the great strength of capitalism in the United States, growing out of our civil war for liberty and equality, and then of the huge sums contributed in my own Wisconsin by taxpayers for the free and universal education of all the workers, from the primary school to the state university. My British trade-union hearers were surprised and eagerly inquisitive. They had thought of us as only a money-grabbing people. To me, their awakening by my speech was pitiful.

The dining and junketing of our delegation to Britain seemed to me a waste of time. The Glasgow city council took us on a two-day trip to Loch Lomond and the Rob Roy country. I was thrilled, but it was not my idea of investigation. We were supposed to find out the political and labor conditions which made the municipal ownership of public utilities apparently so successful in England and Scotland, while it was, in the United States, so often a failure.

But the dining and junketing turned out to be a rare opportunity to study personalities. I started in, during our junkets, to make a census of the aldermen and councillors in the municipalities, as compared with American aldermen in our larger cities. I interviewed councillors regarding themselves and their colleagues, as to their business and labor interests, their places of residence, their wealth and employment, their political affiliations. Strangely enough, I found only one councillor whom I could identify as the "labor fakir" so familiar to me. The Tories of Liverpool had nominated him to capture the labor vote. I turned my census over to Frank J. Goodnow, member of our British delegation, at that time professor of political science at Columbia University and

later president of Johns Hopkins University. He had been
selected by both sides to write the report on the British
Municipality. His conclusions, incorporating my "statistics," were that the British municipalities were governed
by the "upper classes"—the business men, the financial
men, the professional men, the "gentlemen."

I was not yet satisfied with my investigation of town
councillors. I wanted to sit down with the Glasgow councillors. I took a week's trip from London to Glasgow, in
the interval before sailing for America. The town council
was a business man's dining club and chamber of commerce. I turned up every day at the free lunch, furnished
by the municipality in the town hall, the only compensation received by the councillors for their services. What a
stir of "graft" this daily free lunch would have created
in America! I sat mainly with the committee having
charge of the street railways. There daily the general manager, Mr. Dalrymple, appointed by this committee of
councilmen, showed up to talk over his operations. With
him I visited the greater part of the plant, and talked
with his subordinates. Dalrymple was called to Chicago
by the advocates of municipal ownership in that city, and,
much to their confusion, reported against municipal ownership in Chicago. Well, I could see why. In his own street
railway in Glasgow, his board of directors was strictly a
business concern to which he reported daily. He alone
made appointments of subordinates. There was no need
of an American civil service law.

In Chicago our delegation spent a day with Samuel
Insull, head of the private electric works. He proudly
showed us around what I became convinced was the best

up-to-date plant of its kind that we visited in England or America. He had been trained by Edison. He knew how to deal with the Chicago politicians. Insull was the American Dalrymple. When, twenty-seven years afterwards, at the age of seventy-four, he was fleeing across the Mediterranean and convoyed home by vindictive America, I stood up for him, with my conservative friends, as the victim of American capitalism which compelled him to extend his plant or be crushed by competitors, and which furnished him easy money. This had been urged upon him by the bankers who profited by selling his securities to the widows and orphans. My view was institutional. They wanted a goat for the sins of capitalism. I would regulate but not destroy the system. They would punish the victims of the system. Why punish one victim while others get away with the profits? I could only be sorry over the tragedy of a great American, as I saw him at the age of forty-seven, becoming a scapegoat for America at the age of seventy-four.

Well, I had my own professorial tragedy at the age of forty-five. Mr. Sullivan and I agreed that we would write separate reports and then exchange them through the central office of Mr. Maltbie in New York. I wrote my report on the ship returning from England, but waited for Sullivan's report before finishing it. His Labor Report came through to me, and, with it before me, I finished my report on Labor and Politics and sent it to Maltbie's office to be transmitted to Sullivan. But it never was transmitted to him. I had pointed out my differences and had criticized his report, but he had no opportunity to reply and to criticize my report, until after the volume was printed.

Then he printed, on his own account, a large-sized pamphlet. I was charged with the most heinous offenses, with lack of good faith, with underhanded investigations of my own without allowing him to be present—in short, with everything that would disgrace a university professor. I first learned of this reply from my students while at Pittsburgh with them on the Pittsburgh Survey. A glance at it terrified me. I could think of no answer. The pamphlet was to be sent to all university libraries, all faculties of political economy, and all participants in our Civic Federation investigation. I decided I must leave Pittsburgh that night and go home to Madison. My students there tried to quiet me down. But all of the sleepless way home I saw that I must resign from the University, and that everything I had done must be discredited. I met my wife at the door, exclaiming to her that all was over and I was ruined. As soon as I could tell her what had happened she replied merely that I had forgotten. She did not know exactly what I had forgotten, but she went to work on all of my correspondence, made out her memoranda, and packed it all in a suitcase for me to take to the New York headquarters, to ask for an investigation by the Civic Federation. I was in suspense, and was even more humiliated when our chairman, Mr. Ingalls, said briefly, in presiding at the meeting, that this dispute between Commons and Sullivan was only a personal matter, and did not concern the commission.

What happened was that the clerk in Maltbie's office had overlooked the arrangement that my report was to be sent to Sullivan. Instead, it had been sent directly to the printer. My wife was right. I had forgotten that ar-

rangement with Sullivan. Neither of us knew of that
oversight in Maltbie's office.

Thus ended the big tempest in my little teapot. I never
heard from anybody anything about Sullivan's attack. I
tell it as a warning to my secretaries and Friday Niters,
and as a proof of the tragedies I go through on account
of my "forgetter."

It was in the midst of winding up this Civic Federation
report that I worked during six months on the public
utility law in McCarthy's "bill factory." I adopted nearly
the whole of the recommendations signed by nineteen of
the twenty-one members of the investigating committee of
the Civic Federation. I did not, of my own initiative, introduce anything new in drafting the bill. I got it all from
others. I was a kind of sieve for funnelling ideas from
everywhere into legislative enactment. Here was, however, my first opportunity to get legal ideas. I had taken
one lecture course at Johns Hopkins on the history of real
estate law. That had been my legal preparation. My
Civic Federation colleagues were engineers, general man-
agers, publicists. But here, in Wisconsin, we had to fit
those recommendations into the decisions of the Supreme
Court of the state and of the United States.

I went first to Chief Justice Winslow of the Wisconsin
Court. He typified the Wisconsin spirit of an independent
judiciary. I had seen with pity in my own Indiana a justice
of the State Supreme Court, a friend of mine and of my
family, hanging sheepishly around the State Republican
Convention seeking a renomination. But Winslow was a
Democrat, a man of notable personality, who served for

twenty-nine years on the supreme bench of a state over-
whelmingly Republican. At one period a majority of the
justices were Democrats elected by popular vote. The
judiciary were "out of politics." I traced this unusual fact
to the electoral system of the state. At an early date the
election of all judges had been placed at the spring elections, when township, county and city officers and local
boards of education were elected. The judicial candidates
were nominated by petition, and their names were placed
alphabetically on the voters' ballots. The people of Wisconsin always point to the high character and ability of
their judges and the prompt administration of justice. The
"machinery" of election or appointment, however, was
just as important as the "spirit" of the people. This I
learned over and over, during my thirty years in Wisconsin, beginning with the civil service law in 1905. It was
this experience that I tried to formulate, during the twenty-
five years following the public utility law of 1907, into a
theory of institutional economics, whose basic principles
are collective action and personality.

Justice Winslow could not help me on the public utility
legislation, because, as he said, the law would come before
him for adjudication. I asked him whom he would recom-
mend. He named Harry L. Butler, of Madison, as a leading constitutional lawyer in the state. Butler was known
as a "corporation lawyer." He often appeared before the
State and Federal Supreme Courts representing the largest
combinations of capital in the United States. He was a
Democratic Conservative; I was a La Follette Progressive.
I explained to him the general outline of what I wanted to
do, derived from my public utility investigations. I found

that he was wholly in sympathy with the proposals, and he started me off with what I might expect the courts to decide on the various points raised in the proposed legislation. Since then I have always conferred with him or have heard him analyze and criticize most of the constitutional questions brought up in current legislation or court decisions. From him I learned to know in advance what the judges would do. He was afterwards employed by the joint legislative committee on workmen's accident compensation as their legal counsel, where he introduced what seemed to me the most ingenious legal devices to make that law constitutional.

On one occasion, after the War, involving the Standard Oil Company, Butler said to me, "You cut me out of a juicy fee." I had argued to the directors of the company and their lawyer, at a private conference in their hotel at Madison, that, although I knew the Supreme Court of the United States would decide in their favor on the issue of discrimination then at stake between them and their small competitors, the latter supported by the Attorney General and the State Market Commission, yet the Supreme Court was usually fifteen years behind the times. Meanwhile, it was to the interest of the company directors to keep their unpopular corporation out of politics and not to bring the Supreme Court into further disrepute by driving it to make what they knew would be a decision in their favor. They should come forward and make a voluntary public announcement, at a conference of the big and little oil companies with the Attorney General, accepting the particular piece of regulation which the Market Commission and the Attorney General were then demanding.

Their lawyer asked me one question: "Are economists opposed to big business?" I answered, "Not if they get big by efficiency and not by discrimination." The lawyer made the voluntary announcement at the conference that same day, crediting it to my suggestion that morning at the hotel. That is how Harry Butler learned that I had cut him out of a juicy fee.

The Attorney General, Herman L. Ekern, a leading La Follette progressive, also earned my lasting admiration. He might have gone ahead and issued the order anyhow, notwithstanding the unexpected voluntary concession of the Company, as he was insistently urged to do by his deputies. He could then have been elected governor, whether he won out or was defeated in the ensuing legal battle. This also I had pointed out to the Company representatives. But Ekern did not "play politics." He accepted, in good faith, this voluntary offer of big business, and lost the nomination for governor.

Possibly I went too far in my final generalizations on collective bargaining instead of legislation, based on these few experiences of mine. In this case the conflicting interests were, on the one hand, the Standard Oil Company owning at least two-thirds of the filling stations in the state, and, on the other hand, the little establishments and the farmers' coöperatives. They met together in several conferences, with the State of Wisconsin, through its Attorney General and Market Commission. There was no legal contest about rights or constitutionality, although public hearings, according to "due process," had been held throughout the state and much publicity had been given to the issue. There was simply a private but not secret conference of the conflicting interests, who reached a voluntary agreement with a public-spirited state official.

My capable university assistant, Donald Montgomery, who had helped me on the Pittsburgh Plus case, and had then been appointed investigator for the State Market Commission, went ahead, after the Standard Oil case, to investigate and promote similar voluntary arrangements in other industries of the state. He was making good progress, but a political reaction with a different governor lost him his job. He landed immediately with the Federal Trade Commission, though regretting his inability to carry the collective-bargaining principle further in Wisconsin. After an interval of two years and a change back to the Progressives, another graduate of the University was appointed to continue Montgomery's work. But eventually he found that his work was taken over by the National Industrial Recovery Administration.

So, perhaps my generalizations on collective bargaining in place of legislation were too sweeping, though I hoped they were only premature. Much depends on politics and the accidents of personality in the executive, legislative and judicial branches of government. I perceived that Marx's class struggle and dictatorship were more dramatic and appealing than the quiet and patient investigations and collaborations of collective bargaining. Even in democratic America I see how quickly a private citizen, when elected or appointed to public office, becomes a bureaucrat. He thinks, as somebody said of Noah, that because he knows a thing or two he knows it all. He is the germ of dictatorship, unwilling to yield his authority in the slow process of negotiating with conflicting interests and letting them get the credit of bringing about a reasonable

understanding among themselves. So I get back again to
the personalities of leadership.

In the negotiations leading up to the public utility law
of 1907, the joint legislative committee did not rely so
much upon public hearings required by "due process of
law," where everybody has a lawful right to be heard and
the conflicting opinions are irreconcilable, as upon private
and even confidential conferences with the leaders of the
interests to be brought under the law, where concessions
could be made and the investigations of experts could be
weighed in the balance. It was this general class of negotiations which I afterwards defined as "rationing transactions," distinguished from managerial and bargaining
transactions.

Outstanding personalities, from whom I derived my
ideas, come to my mind. There were Mr. C. B. Winslow,
the legal representative, apparently, of most of the public
utility corporations. He kept them all informed of the
progress of the negotiations and the attitudes of various
participants. There was Senator A. W. Sanborn, from
Ashland, formerly judge in a circuit court, afterwards
chairman of the joint interim committee which drafted the
workmen's accident compensation law. From him I got
the idea, thrilling to me at that time, of legal valuations
in economics as always looking toward the future. From
this starting point I worked for many years in making
Futurity the main principle of economics, distinguished
from all the schools of economic thought which based
their theories on past labor or present feelings. Sanborn's
futurity became my connecting link between law, ethics,
psychology, and economics.

There was also Senator W. H. Hatton, a wealthy lum-

berman, who to my thinking was the most capable negotiator in my experience, though I was told by another
lumberman that he had not become as wealthy as he
might have become, with the opportunities he had in the
pine forests. Hatton had been chairman of the Senate
Committee in 1905. For about five months this committee
had La Follette's railroad bill in its keeping, with a
majority against the bill. Hatton was a Progressive, and
during that five months he negotiated the committee into
framing the bill which was adopted by the legislature and
signed by Governor La Follette.

The Railroad Commission, appointed under that law of
1905 by La Follette and confirmed by the Senate, was a
notable body of men. At every step in framing the public
utility law of 1907 I submitted matters to them. I could
tell beforehand, and so could the legislative committee,
just how the Railroad Commission would administer and
interpret the public utility law. This foreknowledge enabled us greatly to condense the bill, leaving a huge field
of investigation and discretion to the Commission, instead
of inserting in the law the multitude of minute details, so
familiar and so often conflicting in American legislation.
There were on the Commission Judge Barnes, a Democrat,
afterwards elected to the Supreme Court of the state;
B. H. Meyer, afterwards taken away from Wisconsin to a
position on the Interstate Commerce Commission; Hal-
ford Erickson, La Follette's Commissioner of Labor and
Statistics who had furnished him with the mass of statistics
on railways which La Follette put across to the people in
the three-hour speeches of his campaigns. The people of
Wisconsin became certainly the best-educated people in
the United States on statistics, and La Follette the first and

only politician in the United States, to my knowledge, who could hold a popular audience for hours on that branch of economics so disgustedly avoided by college students. Erickson was not renominated by Governor Philipp, and, after setting up a consulting office in Chicago, he became affiliated with the Byllesby Management Corporation, operating public utilities in several states.

With such a body of men for my teachers in law, economics, and statesmanship, I was completing my graduate studies, left unfinished at Johns Hopkins University. One night, when I left a conference at midnight on my bicycle, going to my family in our summer cottage on the lake, I was arrested by a policeman and had to pay a fine and costs the next morning at eight o'clock. Senator La Follette, on hearing the story, said, "You plaster the State with laws and the State fines you for doing it." Well, I was only paying tuition for the best university education I ever had. I gained quite a reputation with my bicycle and, years later, with my auto, as a law-breaker. My name was headlined in the papers. Often I was treated rough, until, as the chief of police told me, he had called his policemen down for rough-housing men who were better educated than they were. The matter settled into routine, and my secretary planned to appear in police-court at eight o'clock and pay one dollar and costs without putting up any argument. The policemen, too, became gentle and friendly, and politely called me "professor" while handing me their calling card. It was a beautiful system of registration and tuition.

I learned one big thing. I started, in 1907, what I have been told was the first university course in the country on the subject of municipal public utilities. My associate in the course was M. S. Dudgeon, of McCarthy's legal staff, with whom I had worked the preceding spring on the public utility laws. I had learned much of the technique of running down decisions of the Supreme Courts on the problem of "reasonable value." But I wanted to hear Dudgeon work the whole thing out from the earliest history of the common law. He took the legal aspects and I the economic aspects of reasonable value. The first class numbered fifteen students. Eventually several of them earned national reputations in that field, some in the employment of regulatory commissions, others employed as economists by large private concerns. I started also a graduate research course on "Value and Valuation" and a lecture course on "Public Value," both of which I have continued to the present time. Here I worked out a comparison of legal and economic theories of value. My students were given topics requiring them to work in the offices of the Railroad Commission, latterly the Public Service Commission, where they were generously received, and many of them afterwards were appointed to permanent positions until they were drawn away by private interests. The Railroad Commission became their laboratory. Soon I turned over the "public utility" course to another member of the faculty. It finally landed in the hands of my present colleague in the department, Martin G. Glaeser, a member of my first class of fifteen, who now lectures to a hundred and fifty or more undergraduate and graduate students.

I came to Wisconsin in 1904 to write a history of labor in the United States. My above-mentioned work with the

WIFE, JACK, RACHEL, 1904

legislatures in 1905 and 1907 was outside this field. I could not bring my students into that work with me because I was there getting a new education myself. Not until I started the course on public utilities with Dudgeon, in the fall of 1907, did I know enough, or have acquaintance enough with the leaders, to bring university students into the subject. And then, after one semester, I turned that course over to others. Somehow it has always been that way. When a subject became routine I lost initiative. I liked to see somebody else do it. Only while it was new, uncertain, risky, could I get up enough volition to make me go. I learned afterwards, from the physical scientist, C. S. Peirce, the founder of American "pragmatism," that the proper name for it was "the irritation of doubt." It had been called "the instinct of curiosity." Whatever it was, many years afterwards, in 1933, I incorporated it in economic theory by broadening the economist's doctrine of "limiting and complementary factors" into the behavioristic doctrine of "strategic and routine transactions." I wanted to work on strategic factors. I could turn over to my students the routine work, hoping that some of them, at least, would rise to the irritation of doubt. The bulk of the world's work is, of course, routine. The problem of education is how to jerk up routine into the irritation of doubt. When it came to drafting the Industrial Commission law in 1910, I had fifty undergraduates speaking a half-dozen languages, supervised in groups by graduates. They were charting up, in large sheets hung on the walls, the labor laws of all countries. Quite a number of them came through with the excited question, "What does it all mean?" Well, I could only

say to all of them: "What it means is what it means for
Wisconsin. That is what I am trying to find out. Dig
it up for yourselves, and hand me in a topic telling me
what you find and what you think it means for Wisconsin."

This is the way I did my labor history. The work
stretched over a period of thirty years, in ten volumes of
documents and three volumes of text, the third volume
only just now coming out when I can no longer work.
All of it has been done by my students—formerly graduate
students, now my colleagues in the department. I encouraged them, all these thirty years, by saying to them
as occasion arose: "I am not a person; I am a syndicate.
I tell the world of you."

Yet, I do not think that I neglected details. They were
forced on me by Easley. I was happy one time when he
encouraged me by saying, "You are the only one I have
had who could stick to details and make generalizations
at the same time." Always I tried, one way or another, to
get my students to see that details and their meanings are
science. It is the meanings of details that get you out of
routine. I have often spent much time with an entire class
in puzzling over a new detail which one of them discovered. Often they compelled me to change my theories.
Details are usually known as "facts"; their meanings are
science.

I had to work out a time-schedule in order to do it.
When I worked in the printing office I went to bed at four
A.M. When I puzzled over the meanings of details I got
out of bed at 4 A.M. Then I would spring on my students
a new theory. I remember how this eccentricity disturbed

Mr. Walsh when I was a member of the Industrial Relations Commission. He said to the Commission, "You never can tell what Commons will spring on us the next morning." Neither could I.

My teaching on labor subjects, beginning in 1904 with twenty-five or thirty students, was expanded and specialized during the years, until, in order to keep down my hours of teaching I contrived a two-year sequence for juniors and seniors. The courses were mainly lectures. The sequence and specialization were labor unions, labor legislation, labor management, immigration. Eventually it was possible to turn over these specialized courses to my own former graduates, until we had, including myself, five specialists as colleagues in the one field of labor within the economics department. These specialists greatly expanded the details and worked out their own meanings. They could not, of course, give all of their time to the one subject of "labor." Yet it is surprising how, from John Locke to Adam Smith, to Ricardo, Proudhon and Karl Marx, it is possible to build a whole system of political economy on the one foundation of labor. I, too, found this to be true in my *History of Labor in the United States*. The reason, I discovered, was that the word Labor has as many meanings as you wish to read into it. Some of my capitalist friends even speak of "capital labor." Eventually I learned to avoid these multiple meanings by substituting "managerial transactions" for "labor," "bargaining transactions" for wages, and "rationing transactions" for collective labor.

This practice, in the University of Wisconsin, of building up a faculty of teachers from among the professor's own students, has often been criticized by means of the obnoxious analogy, "inbreeding." I have found two excuses in my experience. The State of Wisconsin is a small state of only two and a half million people—less than the population of many cities. Its wealth and tax-paying ability are far down in the list of states. Yet, in proportion to population or wealth, the state has long paid more for its state university than other states. But it cannot compete with the outstanding privately endowed universities or with private business, which pay two or three times the Wisconsin salaries. Neither can the University, with its low salaries in comparison, pull teachers with established reputations away from other universities. Consequently we have to run our own seed-bed for future professors, and take them when they are young. Curiously enough, our own product will often stay with us, notwithstanding offers of several thousand dollars more elsewhere. I figured this out and often illustrated it to my students according to the legal theory of value of service. The legal theory was formulated by the American, Henry C. Carey, and taken over by the Frenchman Frederic Bastiat, as early as the year 1850. It was rejected by economists as "optimistic" and superficial. What is a professor "worth" to the university? He is worth as much as he can get elsewhere. How much does a professor donate to the university? He donates as much as the excess salary he could get elsewhere. Superficial indeed! Opportunistic, indeed, instead of fundamental, like labor, or pain, or pleasure. Yet it is the business man's theory of value, taken over by the courts from the customs of business. And it is the professor's theory and the laborer's theory when he is forced to

choose between better or worse alternatives. It is a behavioristic theory of value.

In my own case I found that I had been acting on this
theory of value all along. I came to the University in
1904 at the same salary, $3,000, which I had been getting
from the Civic Federation. That was all I was worth, and
even more than I was worth, to the University. The University paid only one-half of it; Professor Ely raised the
other half from donations by private capitalists. The latter thought, perhaps, that I might be worth what the Civic
Federation, another association of capitalists, was paying
me. Yet I got certain "intangible values" by making the
change. I was only too glad to get the new opportunity
of writing a labor history. So I figured that I was *donat-
ing* nothing to the University.

My second excuse for "inbreeding" was to deny the
accusation. My students who took over my work had
spent from two to seventeen years in other work and in
labor investigations or administration, outside the University, before they were called to teaching positions. Indeed,
I always insisted that students should go out and find jobs
for themselves in industry if they had not already done
so, before finishing their graduate studies. I told them of
my own hobo days. When they came back they knew
more than I did about "labor." They taught me. They
kept me up-to-date. A kind of "natural selection" ensued.
If they found this manual labor too hard, or did not like
to work with "hunkies," they dropped out of my classes.
Those who remained had so often corrected my mistakes,
or compelled me to revise my theories, or showed me
where I was obsolete, or had set up their own theories,

that I could see no "inbreeding" of ideas. It was the other way round.

This was true when I started my labor history in 1904. I found John B. Andrews and Helen L. Sumner, the one from Dartmouth, the other from Vassar. They were eager to go out exploring with me. They had the irritation of doubt. We spent about three years together hunting documents, old labor papers, early correspondence, and then bringing them back to Madison in the original or in typewritten copies. Here we settled down, with other students, to figure out what they all meant.

For these first three years I spent one semester at Madison, and had the other eight months for travel. My students and I, in our first year, scoured the libraries at Madison and Chicago for everything written or published on labor in the United States. We devised a system of 4 x 6 cards on which each of us indexed, with comments, all of the topics, all of the persons, all of the books and libraries, which we might need. The 4 x 6 catalogue grew, during fifteen years, into a big filing case built for the purpose. This was housed at first in the Wisconsin Historical Library, then in the John R. Commons Labor Research Library. I can tell, by the handwriting on the cards, who were the students in successive generations who left their mark on that index. For me, it is more than a library catalogue. It is alive with personalities, with trips that we took, with vivid interviews, with detective work in running down clues, with the excitement of discovery. I have many stories that I tell of John and Helen persistently following clues into the sand forests of Jersey or the attics of forgotten heirlooms from Boston to Tennessee or Kansas. Indeed, when in my seclusion I now devour detective novels, I recognize my search for clues. I even tell my Friday Niters that if I were to start over again in teaching economics, my first textbook would be a detective novel.

We discovered, from reading McMaster's *History of the People of the United States,* that there had been published in New York, in 1834, a daily labor paper, *The Man.* It was said to have been the second penny daily published in this country, the first, a few months before, being *The Sun.* Nobody had seen the labor paper. McMaster quoted it from other newspapers. We put *The Man* on our finding list. Eventually I discovered its title in the hand-written catalogue of the library of the New York Historical Society. I rushed to the librarian. He said that paper was covered up by the accumulation of seventy years of newspapers, and could not be gotten out. I found, from him, that Cornelius Vanderbilt had promised the Historical Society a new building for its archives. I visited my friend from Civic Federation days, V. Everit Macy, a donor of $10,000 to the expenses of my labor history, and a friend of Cornelius. I asked him if he could get Cornelius to bring pressure upon the librarian. He did. The librarian put two men in overalls to work for two weeks, excavating for *The Man.* They found him. I went over the paper eagerly, covering the fourteen months of its earthly life. I marked items and pages to be copied. I put in a typewriter for three months. Practically everything worth while from that ancient *Man* was brought back to Madison. I felt like an archæologist in Egypt, confronted by an Arabian bashaw refusing to let him dig for the relics of bygone Pharoahs, but able to bring him to terms by the pressure of American Capitalism.

Afterwards I met McMaster and told him of my digging for *The Man*. He told me of a similar experience, twenty years earlier, with the older brother of my bashaw. McMaster had found a daily paper. He worked on it until about eleven o'clock when the bashaw said he had to close up for two hours on account of lunch. McMaster lunched him and champagned him, and came back. He worked until five P.M. The librarian said it was closing time. McMaster said he would come the next morning. The librarian said a non-member could not come more than one day without a letter of introduction from a member. It was summer time and all members were out of town. Finally McMaster located one at Trenton, New Jersey. He made the trip, got the letter, and thereafter took the librarian out every noon for champagne and lunch. In those early days of historical exploration McMaster smoothed the sheik-librarians with toxicants and I smoothed them with capitalists. It depended on the depth of the excavations.

Professor Ely had solicited $30,000 for our labor history. The donors were V. Everit Macy, afterwards president of the National Civic Federation, and foremost in other civic work in New York; Stanley McCormick, friend of my earlier backer, William English Walling; R. Fulton Cutting, the New York lawyer, famous for his public-spirited work in New York and the nation; Captain Ellison A. Smyth, textile capitalist in South Carolina, whose notable community work for his employees Professor Ely had previously written up; Justice P. Henry Dugro, of

New York; State Senator William H. Hatton of Wisconsin; Charles R. Crane of New York. Professor Ely had himself published a volume on the Labor Movement in 1886, when the Knights of Labor were at their height. We thought, at first, that the libraries of Wisconsin, and especially the John Crerar Library at Chicago, where Professor Ely's large collection was located, along with a search in other libraries, might furnish us with material for the history. But Andrews, Miss Sumner, and I found so much additional material and so much that was not known to historians, that we decided to publish first the selected documents. Professor Ely arranged with the A. H. Clark Company, of Cleveland, Ohio, to bring these out in ten volumes. Thus appeared, in 1910, our *Documentary History of American Industrial Society,* edited by myself and five associates. It was not until 1918 that the two volumes of *History of Labour in the United States* by "Commons and Associates" were published. The associates were my graduate students.

The publication of the *Documentary History* exhausted the original donations and we were compelled to obtain funds elsewhere. Andrew Carnegie had established a large fund for studies and publications on American history. The labor history had been placed in the hands of Carroll D. Wright, Commissioner of Labor. He had arranged with me to write one of the chapters. Upon his death, in 1909, I understood that about $7,000 remained from the Carnegie fund, for all purposes; but the work was not yet finished. Professor H. W. Farnam, of Yale University, came forward with the offer to furnish $25,000 in order to finish the Carnegie program. Farnam created

the Board of Research Associates in American Economic
History of which I was a member for the field of labor.
This connection enabled me to obtain funds not only to
complete the first two volumes of the labor history in
1918, but to supplement, by $10,000, the larger amount
furnished by the University of Wisconsin for completing
the third volume, just now in process of publication for
1935. The first two volumes brought the history down
to the year 1897, but we considered that the history following that year belonged to "current labor problems,"
and this is the title of the third volume. It is the period
of nearly forty years during which I myself have participated. As I now go over the manuscripts of my colleagues in the department, formerly my own students, who
are preparing this third volume, I am again excited, this
time by seeing myself in action during forty years and
coming toward me out of the past as I look from my rock-
ing-chair upon the panorama of Lake Mendota.

I had known Professor Farnam, at a distance, in the
meetings of the American Economic Association. He had
written his dissertation while a student in Germany, on a
subject in the field of labor. At a meeting of the Economic Association at Baltimore, in 1906, there was
formed, upon the inspiration of Professor Ely, the American Association for Labor Legislation. Farnam was made
president and I was made secretary, with headquarters at
Madison. I made John B. Andrews my "executive secretary," to do all the work, and associated with him Irene
Osgood, graduate student, as assistant. It turned out that
they teamed up for life. My office earned quite a reputation during thirty years as a preparation for home eco-

nomics. John and Irene financed themselves for the Association for Labor Legislation by making investigations for the Wisconsin Department of Labor and the United States Department of Labor. John investigated the manufacture of phosphorous matches throughout the country and drafted the bill, afterwards adopted by Congress, for taxing out of existence the manufacture of phosphorous matches. He and Irene arranged a program for the first meeting of the Association at Atlantic City with the American Economic Association. Professor Farnam presided. He said to me, while strolling down the famous "board walk" of Atlantic City, "I am so enthusiastic about this first year's work that I will give $5,000 a year to bring Andrews to New York and set up there the headquarters of the Association." Then he went on: "Curious, isn't it, that you, a radical, and I, a conservative, find ourselves working together." It was curious, but good for me during all the remaining years of Farnam's life.

I sometimes wondered, while Selig Perlman was writing of the Homestead Strike for our Labor History, whether I would be biased in favor of Carnegie, when I had been financed, in part through Farnam, by Carnegie's money. For one thing, Carnegie had advocated a fifty per cent inheritance tax on great wealth. That suited me. I could always say to my conservative friends, who protested loudly against my radical views on the subject, "I am satisfied to go as far as Carnegie." I was told that Carnegie had given away, during his lifetime, so many millions of dollars that he died a poor man with only ten million.

Then, again, I always found in myself a bushwacking

admiration for great warriors, great desperadoes, great
captains of industry, who could hold up a stagecoach or
a nation or the whole system of capitalism. I was never a
pacifist. I think it came from that original sin of my
childhood, which, I have already confessed, brought my
mother to tears. Carnegie certainly held up the entire
steel industry of the country through the financiers led
by the House of Morgan, when he sold to them, for something like 447 million dollars, a property that would cost
for reconstruction probably less than 100 million dollars.
He had created for himself the strategic position in the
new technology. When I heard him, in 1914, testifying
before the Industrial Relations Commission, I saw how
he could do it. He was far ahead of the most scintillating,
adroit and persuasive salesman who had ever put over on
me a real estate proposition. Even my highly successful
lawyer friend, Frank P. Walsh, who had saved eighteen
men from the gallows and now was chairman of the
Commission, could do nothing with him on cross examination. He maneuvered Walsh like a little boy. I just sat
there and enjoyed Carnegie—a laughing Robin Hood of
the capitalist system.

Then, too, I previously had been given a chance to study
Carnegie in his original Sherwood Forest of Pittsburgh.
In 1906 Mr. Devine, editor of *Charities and the Commons,*
came to me at Madison and asked if I would take supervision of the labor end of a Pittsburgh Survey, to be
financed by the Russell Sage Foundation and headed up in
the field by Paul U. Kellogg. After the Pittsburgh Survey
Devine's magazine changed its name to *The Survey,* and
Kellogg became its editor. I accepted Devine's invitation,

with the provision that I could arrange my trips to Pittsburgh during University vacations and examination periods. I took with me three of my students. Two of them, William M. Leiserson and John A. Fitch, did the work. The third was not interested. For the first month I asked them not to ask any questions but to go around with me and see me interview. Fitch was from the prairies of South Dakota and thought that labor leaders had the horns which he had known in action on the farm. He was surprised to find that the principal labor leader was a Sunday School superintendent. Others were Christian gentlemen. He remained in Pittsburgh for a year, and the Russell Sage Foundation published his book on *The Steel Worker*. Afterwards he became the economist on the faculty of the New York School of Social Work.

Leiserson was from the sweatshops of the New York East Side, and he made the survey of all the unskilled and common laborers. We three ate and lived together, reviewing their own and my interviews. We arranged a scheme of 4 x 6 cards in triplicate, one to go to the Russell Sage Foundation, one to me and one kept by the interviewer. I had a mass of these cards for lectures to my class at Madison. I took others of Kellogg's staff around with me. Crystal Eastman's subject was accidents, and her book on that subject was published by the Russell Sage Foundation.

Here I learned my first lesson in accident prevention. The United States Steel Company was then just becoming a pioneer in this field. I followed this up and, when I became a member of the Wisconsin Industrial Commission, I attended conferences of the safety experts of the

Steel Corporation brought together from different parts of the country. I decided then that a workman's accident compensation law, if properly drawn, would cost nobody anything. It would not raise prices for the consumers, and would actually increase the profits of the employers. It was amazing to me how greatly accidents could be prevented by safety experts if employers could be furnished an inducement to hire them for the purpose. I wanted all employers to be compelled by law to pay accident compensation as an inducement to accident prevention. Afterwards, in 1911, in drafting the Industrial Commission law for Wisconsin, I tied together, under one administrative body, the workmen's insurance and the accident prevention law. These had been conceived, in Wisconsin and other states, as two independent activities under two independent state boards, insurance to be shifted to consumers in higher prices, and safety to be enforced on employers by factory inspectors and criminal prosecutions with jury trials, where the employer was assumed to be innocent unless proved without a doubt to be guilty. Why not assume the opposite? The employer intends to do right but does not have sufficient inducement. Why not shape up legislation and administration on this assumption? Let the state furnish him with the inducements by taxing him proportionate to his employees' loss of wages by accidents, and then employ safety experts, instead of crime detectives and prosecutors, to show him how to make a profit by preventing accidents.

The experts of the Steel Company claimed, to my astonishment, that they could reduce the burden of accidents two-thirds, if they were supported, as they were, by the company. Obviously I wanted all employers to be forced by law to follow the lead of the Steel Corporation, and to make a profit by doing good, instead of defending themselves as alleged criminals for neglecting the safety of their employees.

Eventually, in 1921, I began to extend this principle to unemployment. Why not make individual employers responsible for their own unemployment, instead of so-called "society"? They could then make a profit by hiring employment experts and paying the bills for public employment offices. Eventually I administered such a scheme in the Chicago Clothing Market, and the State of Wisconsin enacted it into law in 1932.

This near thirty years of my own experience, beginning with the Steel Company in 1907, I have written up in my *Institutional Economics*. I was trying to save Capitalism by making it good. It was because I admired, not "capitalism," but great capitalists, as far beyond my own abilities, but wanted to make them as good as the best instead of negligent. Most of them thought, at first, that I was guilty of malpractice.

I wanted also to make trade unions as good as the best of them that I knew. In my Pittsburgh Survey work I interviewed leaders who had been through the Homestead Strike of 1892. One of them, Mahlon Garland, then the collector of customs, took us through the steel works one Sunday night. I wanted to make sure of what I had been told by Mrs. Florence Kelley that men worked twenty-four hours on Sundays in the steel works. Garland pointed to us the place in the mill where he had harangued the strikers who for several months in 1892 had possession of the mills. Several of the workers, now de-unionized, recognized him, and he introduced us to them. They talked freely enough. One of them was a heater, who worked, with blistered face and arms, and against a furnace that reminded me of hell, for twelve hours a day and twenty-four hours every other Sunday when the day and night shifts were changed. He had come on that Sunday morning at about seven o'clock; it was now eleven o'clock at night and he had another eight hours to go. I wish now that I could go back to that furnace and see what has happened since the company started its safety work and installed the eight-hour day. But nobody is admitted any more, as I found when I sent a student, unless the superintendent gets a permit from New York. I did not try to get the permit.

How did this twelve-hour shift and de-unionizing come about? I traced it out in the proceedings of the union. In 1889 the leaders of the union urged their organization to accept the offer of the Carnegie Steel Company to install the eight-hour day. The puddlers and heaters had been operating nine or ten hours. But Carnegie had the patents for the new continuous process that carried the molten iron without cooling from the blast-furnace to the finished steel. He had to operate either an eight-hour or a twelve-hour shift. The union refused in 1889, but Carnegie stirred the nation in 1892 when he wiped out the union and installed the twelve-hour shift. He was then in position, eight years later, in the year 1900, to hold up the steel industry of the United States for 447 million dollars.

I often compare with my students the two industries that I know best, steel and printing. The typographical union, in 1895, made an arrangement with the owners of the linotype patent to install the new machine if their members could have a preference in learning the job and an eight-hour day. The contrast turned on leadership at the strategic point of time. No wonder that eventually I made strategic and routine transactions the basis of my negotional theory of political economy. The two unions were confronted by the new industrial revolution of the past fifty years. What they did fifty years ago, in meeting the new opportunities, laid down the working rules for thousands of workers in the years to follow. Here am I, at seventy-one years of age, with my emeritus salary of $2,000 at the University augmented by $3,000 from my Carnegie pension. The pension goes back to the events of 1889, 1892, and 1900. I guess I am an opportunist.

I tried out this opportunistic theory of value on a labor controversy in Wisconsin, and it ended in an investigation of me by the State Senate. The theory came from Henry C. Carey, as I have stated above regarding a professor's salary. The Russell Sage Foundation, which had financed the Pittsburgh Survey, had now investigated the "loan shark" evil. After several years the Foundation had espoused a remedy. It was found that wage-earners, and other poor people reduced to the level where they could not borrow money in any other way, were paying at a rate as high as 100, 200, or more per cent per year to loan sharks. Indeed, I now found, when the issue came up, that I myself had been a loan shark in my printing office days. A fellow printer, needing money immediately and unable to wait until pay-day, would occasionally come to me and offer to sell his "string" for cash at a discount of five to ten per cent below what he could get for it at the next pay-day. I could then paste his string on my own, showing the amount of typesetting I supposedly had done, and collect my claim at the office the next pay-day. This practice became known as salary-buying, and was an historic method of evading the usury laws. Figuring it out, in view of my later investigation of the "small loan law" promoted by the Russell Sage Foundation and enacted in Wisconsin and some twenty other states, I found that, at five or ten per cent per week, I had been receiving interest from my fellow printers at the rate of 250 to 500 per cent per year. The union afterwards prohibited salary-buying by union members, but the practice, in my day, was so general that no ethical consideration entered into it.

The law, devised for the Russell Sage Foundation, legalized a rate of 3½ per cent a month for short terms on loans less than $300, to be charged only by licensed companies under state supervision, and all unlicensed lending prohibited. This amounted to 42 per cent per year, instead of the secret loan-shark rates, disguised as sales, of 100 or more per cent per year.

I tried to expound this opportunistic theory of value to the legislature. The law based upon it appealed to me at once, from my personal knowledge of what wage-earners, without bankable assets, were up against in their small emergency loans. The state was creating for them an opportunity to borrow at 42 per cent instead of 100 per cent or more. But 42 per cent was outrageous in a state which had been working so hard to reduce the extortions of big business. Yet the State Federation of Labor, through its attorney, supported the bill. My old Progressive friend, Henry A. Huber, then become lieutenant governor, took the lead in demanding the repeal of the law. He had introduced, as State Senator, and valiantly supported throughout the state, my first unemployment insurance bill devised in 1921. He now secured the appointment of a senate committee to investigate the sinister influences that were resisting the repeal of the small loan law. He knew that I was one of those influences. I had drafted a bill, then before the legislature, proposing to turn over to a commission, under the banking department, the investigation and fixing of "reasonable rates" and "reasonable practices" of the small loan companies, instead of fixing these by the state legislature. This eventually was done. But meanwhile Governor Huber went after me in a terrifying examination before the senate committee. Was not the Russell Sage Foundation an association of big capitalists? Did I receive any compensation from the Foundation or from the loan companies? How much was my University salary and how much did I earn outside my salary? He believed me when I said I received no compensation whatever for services in anything I had done on this bill. The money, about $3,000, went to pay expenses and compensation for investigators, and came from the loan companies.

A few days later the Senate went into committee of the whole on the bill. Lieutenant-governor Huber attacked me violently and demanded that I be removed from the University. My reply before the Senate was that "I had been fired from three conservative universities and would just as soon be fired by a Progressive legislature in Wisconsin. Let us go on with the merits of the bill." A Progressive senator said to a group of others, "What can you do with that?" At my seventieth anniversary, shortly after, my students spoke of my "courage," and Governor Philip F. La Follette cited this retort of mine as an example. I took a look into my soul. It was the courage of timidity, like a rat chased into a corner. I never was courageous. I was opportunistic, but pushed into danger by experimentation. If physical scientists risk their lives in experiments why should not an economic scientist risk his job? I was testing Carey's and the courts' theory of value in the economists' laboratory. I continued to support Henry Huber. He and I, with four of my former students—Harold Groves, Paul Raushenbush, Elizabeth Brandeis, Harry Weiss—stood around Governor La Follette to see him sign the unemployment insurance bill, first introduced by Senator Huber twelve years before and now put across by these students. Phil gave me his fountain pen with his name stamped on it in gold.

Victor Berger had founded, in 1898, the Social Democratic Party as a protest against Daniel De Leon and his Socialist Labor Party. De Leon had turned over to me for our Labor History his entire official correspondence. I had known of him since 1889 and known him personally afterwards in his years of extreme poverty. He was, to my notion, the truest interpreter of Karl Marx, but he originated also the idea of two "wings" of the Communist movement, the political party and the industrial union in opposition to the American Federation of Labor. Both Lenin in Russia and W. Z. Foster in America followed De Leon. I stirred up, after the War, some criticism of myself by bringing Foster before my class and introducing him to a mass meeting in the University Armory. But, as I looked at it, Foster, although not a university man, like Marx or De Leon, gave to my class the most scholarly account I have heard of the evolution of communist doctrine from Marx to De Leon and Lenin. De Leon had been a lecturer on international law at Columbia University in the 'eighties, but Foster had worked his way up as a railway employee.

Berger was also an acute "reviser" of Marxian theory, but he would change it from "revolution" to "evolution." Under his leadership the "economic wing" was the existing Wisconsin Federation of Labor, and the "political wing" was the new Social Democratic Party, opposed to De Leon's Social Labor Party and its socialist antagonism to labor unions. Berger was repeatedly a delegate to the conventions of the American Federation of Labor, his "economic wing," where I heard some of his speeches in opposition to Gompers. For the leadership of his political party he converted Eugene Debs to his brand of socialism, while Debs was in jail for violating an injunction issued in the Pullman Strike of 1894. Debs then became repeatedly the Social Democratic candidate for President of the United States.

I had known Debs in my Indiana days of 1893, at his home and extensive library in Terre Haute, when he was secretary of the Railway Fireman's Brotherhood and editor of their official organ. There he expounded to me his plan of the American Railway Union, modeled after the Constitution of the United States, which should include subordinate organizations of all railway employees as "states" in the union. His plan was opposed by the craft-union brotherhoods. Debs separated himself from the Firemen's Brotherhood. Then I heard him soon after, at the convention of his organization in Chicago, 1894, when the Pullman factory workers, organized as one of his "states," came to the session for support of their strike. I was thrilled by his eloquence and his sympathy for the factory employees. I was then a Christian Socialist, my socialism based on Love of Man. Debs pulled off a nation-wide strike of his railway union in sympathy with the Pullman strikers. It was glorious but untimely. President Cleveland sent in the army, the Federal courts issued injunctions, and the Supreme Court confirmed the sentence of Debs to jail for contempt. No wonder that Debs, in jail, was ripe for Berger's political party that would control the appointment of judges in favor of labor unions.

In Wisconsin, during my first fifteen years, I wondered why the socialists in the legislature nearly always lined up with the conservatives against La Follette. After the War they supported the Progressives and La Follette for President, in 1924. La Follette was an extreme individualist, but, at the same time, a strong trade-unionist. I figured it out that the socialists in the legislature during those pre-war years, mainly from Milwaukee, were still following Marx instead of Berger toward the overthrow of capitalism by revolution. They wanted things to get worse before they could get better. But Debs and Berger wanted the condition of labor to get gradually better through a constitutional development of capitalistic institutions. The best "revolutionists" are not paupers. I thought the socialists in the legislature would act differently if they were a majority party, with the responsibilities of office. They did get complete political control of the city of Milwaukee in the election of 1910.

When Berger came to me, after that election, and offered me $6,000 salary, out of which I should pay my personal expenses, if I would make an investigation of the Milwaukee city government with a view to reorganizing it on an efficiency basis, I was eager to accept. But I could not then do so because I could not find a competent executive to organize the investigation under my direction. After six months I discovered that my former student, B. M. Rastall, then with the Extension Division of the University, was willing to resign his position and conduct the Milwaukee investigation. I asked consent of the University President and Regents, stipulating that I should not miss my classes but would use the vacation periods and week-ends. I made a trip to the Chicago and New York private bureaus of municipal research looking for men and methods. Rastall and I brought in, for temporary or permanent work, leading sanitary and other engineers; a young accountant, J. B. Tanner, who afterwards constructed a state budget and cost-system for the legislature of Wisconsin; and F. H. Elwell, afterwards Professor of Accounting in the University. I consulted and submitted our work to Harrington Emerson, the famous efficiency expert, and to Major Charles Hine, organizer of the Consolidated Harriman Railway Lines. I took over to Milwaukee a number of my graduate students. I spent about $30,-000 of the city's money during eighteen months. We made reports and recommendations on cost-systems and organization for several departments of the city government. These included the city incinerator and garbage collection; the water department; consolidation of police alarm and fire alarm telegraph; consolidation of sewer and water excavations from the mains to abutting buildings; a complete reorganization of the health department and city hospitals; employment offices; vocational education; street trades; a municipal reference library like McCarthy's at Madison. We published pamphlet reports and named our organization the Milwaukee Bureau of Economy and Efficiency. Practically all of our recommendations and cost systems were installed by the socialist administration, and I have been told that they have remained to the present day.

It fell to me, when the various recommendations were completed by the staff, to get the socialist administration to adopt and install them. Considerable unrest and criticism soon arose because our Bureau took such a long time to get the reports in shape. The socialist officials and aldermen, to the number of fifty or more, held a caucus every Saturday afternoon to consider and agree upon policies. I appeared at these caucuses, with blue prints and charts, to report progress and answer criticisms. Nearly all of those present were mechanics and tradeunionists. Never before, even in England, had I met such a capable and rational body of men in charge of a city government. I soon discovered that their goal was Efficiency coupled with Service to the poor and the working classes of the city.

During this work of eighteen months I occupied my

early morning hours at the hotel on economic theory. Eventually, in after years, stripping socialism and communism of their various philosophies, I made the one lasting contribution of Karl Marx to economic science a theory of efficiency measured by man-hours instead of dollars. I traced the history of efficiency in economic theory from Ricardo to the modern scientific management. When the conservatives came into power in Milwaukee at the end of two years the Bureau of Economy and Efficiency was abolished. I was politically attacked as an annex to socialism. But, by that time, my skin was thick.

It naturally occurred to me that the State of Wisconsin might set up a State Bureau of Economy and Efficiency. Governor Francis E. McGovern sponsored the idea, in 1911. It was named the Board of Public Affairs, including a budget director, an advisory committee of private organized interests, investigators regarding the resources of the state, and so on. Charles McCarthy captured it for the promotion of the coöperative movement in the state, strongly supported by Governor McGovern. After various legislative changes in subsequent years, what remained of that Board was the budget director.

While working on the public utility law of 1907 I wondered why similar administrative machinery could not be set up for the conflicts of capital and labor. I came across, in the University library, the remarkable volumes by Hector Denis, professor of ethics and economics at the University of Brussels and leader of the socialist group in the Belgian parliament. These volumes, first published in 1897, as *Histoire des Systèmes économiques et socialistes,* enlightened me more than any other history of economic thought. Denis had organized, outside the parliamentary system, the Belgian Superior Council of Labor, composed of representatives of capital, labor and the public, quite similar to Easley's National Civic Federation. It was copied in France.

I immediately set one of my students, Francis H. Bird, from Dartmouth College, to writing for his doctor's dissertation, a history of this Belgian Council. I had an idea that something like this council, based on my experience with the Civic Federation, could be incorporated into a Labor Department for the State of Wisconsin. In 1910, while I was at work on the Milwaukee survey, I placed Bird in charge of organizing my class in labor problems into a miniature world-wide council of capital and labor for the investigation of labor administration in all countries, and then incorporating what fitted the Wisconsin situation into an Industrial Commission law for the state. Then, in drafting such a bill on the initiative of the newly elected governor, Francis E. McGovern, Bird and I joined with McCarthy in his reference library, during the legislative session of 1911. All of the piecemeal labor laws of the state, going back to their beginnings in 1867, and including the new accident compensation law then before the legislature, were now to be brought together under a single council of capital and labor. The older laws were repealed, to take effect when the Commission issued its "orders."

Here the problem was, in part, the constitutional problem, already solved in the railroad commission law, of delegating by the legislature to an administrative body the power to make rules governing, in this case, the relations of employers and employees. The railroad and public utility laws dealt with monopolies. Here we were dealing with competitive industries. In the former laws it had been necessary only to delegate to the Commission authority to investigate, ascertain and fix "reasonable values" and "reasonable services," leaving to the Commission to find out, if it could, what was "reasonable," subject to review by the courts. But in the relation of employers and employees we had to shift the legal meaning of "reasonable" to cover, not values but practices. These practices came under such diverse headings as safety, health, child labor, moral well-being, wage-bargaining, hours of labor, minimum wages for women and children, labor disputes, and free employment offices. Here McCarthy came in with his acute and inescapable criticism. The word "reasonable," under judicial interpretation, meant just ordinary, average, or customary practices, and any effort of the Industrial Commission to raise the standards above that level would be declared by the courts to be unconstitutional as taking the property of employers *without* "due process of law." We spent much time endeavoring to overcome these criticisms by McCarthy. This was my ideal of "collective thinking." We wanted a definition of "reasonableness" that would be acceptable to the courts but would raise the standards above the ordinary. We assigned to Bird the research in law encyclopedias and court decisions to ascertain such a definition. After many conferences he came forward with the definition that reasonableness should mean the *highest* degree of safety, health, well-being of employees, etc., that the nature of the industry or employment would *reasonably permit.*

This definition of reasonableness I worked out afterwards, with my classes, during more than twenty years, as my meaning of "pragmatism" distinguished from "idealism." I find many applications in my *Institutional Economics*. Reasonableness is idealism limited by practicability. Practicability could be investigated and ascertained as actually in operation in the factories of the more progressive employers, and then the rules of the commission, sanctioned by law, could bring other employers up to their level.

Reasonable values and reasonable practices were entirely new words introduced into the theories of political economy. Often my students and sometimes my economist critics said that "reasonable" was something purely subjective, and there were as many meanings of reasonableness as there were individuals. Such a term placed the determination of reasonableness in the arbitrary mind of whatever individual happened to be in authority. But I considered this objection to be an inheritance from the subjective individualism of preceding economic theorists. A collectivistic theory of value derived from existing best practices, from custom, the common law, and the decision of courts, could make reasonableness "objective" and therefore capable of investigation and testimony, leading to the formation of working rules for collective action in control of individual action. I had in mind, all along, the accident prevention work of the United States Steel Corporation, but extended to all other best practices of other pioneer employers. Bird afterwards became labor manager for the United Typothetæ of America, the employers' association in book and job printing; also an adjuster of labor disputes for the War Labor Board, and finally professor of economics in the University of Cincinnati. He sends to me every Christmas a box of Cosmos Club cigars.

But how could the Labor Council of Denis, or the Civic Federation of Easley, be incorporated in the industrial commission law for the investigation of "reasonable" practices? We were afraid that the legislature would provide that future governors, according to American practice, would appoint politicians instead of "industrialists" and trade unionists. The latter could be selected only by their own voluntary associations. Yet these associations could not lawfully select officials of government. So we left that selection to the Commission, and merely provided that the Commission might appoint "advisers without compensation," latterly interpreted by the Attorney General to include necessary expenses. We saw no job-seeking by political parties if there were no money in it from the state treasury. So it turned out. The Commission had, at one time, as many as two hundred advisers, either the well-known leaders themselves, or recommended by the leaders of voluntary associations, including employers, employees, insurance companies, physicians, consumers' leagues, social workers, professors, and others.

It became my assignment, after the Industrial Commission was organized, to initiate these advisory committees, while the other members had charge of the other activities of the commission. I remember my first committee, the committee on boiler safety. There were a manufacturer of boilers, a manufacturer-user of boilers, an insurance company's inspector of boilers, an employee operating boilers, and the deputy of the Commission, a former locomotive engineer who had been a factory inspector in the former labor department. We converted the factory inspectors into secretaries, organizers and investigators for these safety and other committees. The boiler committee met in Milwaukee as often as they decided. I looked in occasionally on their meetings. The Industrial Commission was getting, free of charge, the services of men who could not have been hired at $100 per day by the state and would not have worked at all with a political appointee of the Commission. It required this committee about a year to work out its "boiler code." We considered that, if a committee like this, representing several conflicting economic interests, could agree unanimously upon a code of safety rules, then that code would be considered "reasonable" by the courts. The code would not be "ideal" but it would be pragmatic, the best that the nature of the industry would permit; and it would enlist the better employers to support its enforcement instead of fighting it in the courts. We could always say to employers, "This code is not *our* work nor the work of the legislature. It is the work of your leading fellow employers." And we printed their names when publishing the codes.

Yet "reasonable safety" would be idealistic. It would not be the ordinary safety of the common law, but that ideal safety which was practicable. Boiler manufacturers learned to turn out boilers to meet the specifications of the code. When the code was completed the Commission printed it as a "tentative" code, and held a public hearing —to meet the requirements of "due process of law"— where anybody in the state could appear with his objections. Then the code was referred back to the advisory committee for revision, and the final code, as recommended, was issued as an "order" by the Commission. The old laws on boiler safety were then automatically repealed as dated forward by the enabling act of the legislature, and the new code became the law of the state. Eventually several hundred pages of similar codes, on this and other subjects, with revisions and improvements on earlier codes, were printed by the Commission, and these became, for the lawyers of the state, a part of their working libraries equivalent in authority to the "Wisconsin Statutes," the latter published after each session of the legislature. If a lawyer brought a suit in court involving the unreasonableness of these codes, the legislature had provided that he could bring in no testimony not previously presented to the Industrial Commission, and the court was required to send the case back to the Commission, which meant the advisory committee, to take into account this new testimony and make revision of the code if the committee saw fit. "Reasonableness" was now deemed to be ascertained, not by conflicting arguments and pleadings in court or legislature, nor by legal precedents, nor by ordinary custom, nor by opinions of judges, but by collective action of leading representatives of conflicting interests in the advisory committees. The court passed only on the "due procedure" of the Commission.

After the enactment of the Industrial Commission law in Wisconsin I was called upon at various times to appear before the legislatures, or legislative committees, of Ohio, New York, and Colorado, to explain the principles of the law which was in course of adoption by those states. Lawyers and courts naturally objected to its substitution of business men and labor leaders for lawyers in determining what was reasonable by cross-examinations in a trial court.

It was my participation in these proceedings that set me to investigating what the courts meant by "due process of law." I discovered in the Hurtado case, of 1884, developed in my *Legal Foundations of Capitalism*, that the Supreme Court of the United States changed the meaning of due process from the "due procedure" of the ancient common law to the meaning of "substantial justice" under changing conditions, and that this "justice" was equivalent to reasonableness. So I contended that, in economic conflicts, reasonable values and reasonable practices were not the subjective opinions of anybody, but were the collective opinion, expressed in action, of those whose economic interests were conflicting, but who investigated together and knew by experience all of the facts. This, I found afterwards was Peirce's "pragmatism." My boiler committee was my pragmatism in action. I am now told by a colleague in philosophy that it is "instrumental pragmatism," which philosophers were beginning to formulate. He quotes for me what I wrote in 1913 when I was in the midst of these experiments in methods of teaching economics: "Academic teaching . . . is merely brains without experience. . . . The 'practical' extreme . . . is experience without brains. One is half-baked philosophy—the other is rule-of-thumb."

My colleagues and I, on the Industrial Commission, determined that we must have a deputy who could organize these many safety, health and other committees. Our employer advisers thought we should have a safety engineer who could invent and install safety devices. But we found that their own employees and engineers could originate and install more and better safety devices in their own shops than any outside engineer could possibly contrive for the immense variety of mechanisms throughout the state. What was needed was willingness on the part of employers themselves to have their employees invent safety adjustments of all kinds. We searched the United States for a man who could inspire this willingness. We found him at last in C. W. Price, then with the International Harvester Company. Price was not a technically trained engineer. He had been a "social worker." Yet he knew how to get technicians to work for safety and welfare. He knew the mainsprings of human nature. He was a whirlwind of energy, sagacity, and persuasiveness. He would not, at that time, leave his position with the Harvester Company to accept a political job. But we were able to persuade the company to lend him to us three days a week at $25.00 per day. Price organized safety committees, which always included "welfare," throughout the state and a statewide Conference of Safety. He soon took a permanent position with the Commission, at $3,000 salary, until he went to the National Safety Council to do for the nation what he had been doing for Wisconsin. His work remains, continually expanding, within the state, and the Commission selected as his successor a capable engineer, Mr. R. M. Keown, from the engineering department of the University.

I annexed Price to my classes at the University. He gave me my first idea of the psychology of monotony and routine in modern industry. He aroused Sumner Slichter and found a place for Slichter in one of the plants of the

Harvester Company to work at the machines and study monotony. Out of this study Slichter developed the leading book on Labor Turnover, and eventually landed in the Graduate School of Business Administration at Harvard University.

My appointment to the Industrial Commission was for the two-year term, during which I obtained leave of absence from the University, but continued my research class at evening meetings in my office at the state capitol. My colleague, Joseph E. Beck, holding the six-year term, had been labor commissioner and state statistician under the previous régime of a one-man department. To him naturally fell the organization and direction of the staff in the office and in the field. Eventually he was elected a member of Congress and then was appointed by Governor Philip La Follette as member of the agricultural and marketing commission.

Charles H. Crownhart, the lawyer of the Commission, held the four-year term. To him fell the administration of the new accident compensation law. Beck and I joined in making him chairman. He was the most astute and far-seeing lawyer of all whom I have known. In an accident compensation case where a drunken teamster fell off his truck and was killed, Beck and I, as well as the newspapers and public generally, wished to deny compensation to the widow on the ground that the teamster showed gross negligence by visiting saloons and getting drunk on his employer's time. But Crownhart reasoned that the employer was responsible for employing drunkards as well as unsafe machinery, and that, to hold the employer responsible for employing an unsafe person would be in the public interest of promoting safety by temperance in the industries of the state. The compensation of some $3,000 was awarded to the widow.

I knew that the compensation law would make it more difficult for men over forty years of age to find jobs. But that was another question. Reduce the hours of labor, reduce the speed, in order that the modern factory worker need not be exhausted at forty but could work till seventy, like farmers and professors. Set up old-age pensions and various other correctives. It is, indeed, an endless dilemma that progressive legislation in one direction brings on the need of progressive legislation in other directions. I sympathized with employers who said, "We shall be compelled to discharge our older and less efficient employees, and refuse to employ men out of work." I knew it, but said to them, "You will then be ready to welcome shorter hours, vacations with pay, old-age pensions and other things." Crownhart afterwards was elected a member of the Supreme Court of the State.

My collaboration with these men, with Governor McGovern who appointed us, with the staff of the Commission and with the advisory committees was an all-round education in politics, economics, class conflict, conciliation and administration generally. My fellow workers called me "John" instead of "doc" or "doctor" or professor. These terms of dignity were used by outsiders. My students called me "John R." My letters came addressed to "Hon." We investigated and made findings of fact in important labor disputes where we had compulsory powers of investigation, but no power of compulsory arbitration—to which, in fact, we all were opposed. We held public hearings throughout the state. At one of these hearings, a hundred miles north of Madison, the official reporter of the Commission kindly arranged for me a quick schedule of railway trains. It was about the coldest winter night I had known. I found that I had to change depots twice, get two hours of shivering sleep in a cold hotel, and catch a freight-train caboose at 4 A.M. with a hot stove and board seats in a stuffy room for the train crew. I arrived at my destination a half-hour late with an exploding headache, and stumbled to a seat with the other commissioners. The lawyer for the employer stopped the proceedings and asked who I was. Beck introduced me as Commissioner Commons. After the hearing the lawyer apologized to me. He thought I was a "drunk" who had butted in. Then he took me out for a drink at a swell saloon. So I, a quasi-judicial officer of the law, was suborned by one of the litigants. But it stopped my headache. Then I combed my hair.

When my two-year term on the Industrial Commission was about to expire, Governor McGovern offered to appoint me for the regular six-year term. I gained a reputation by declining a six-year appointment at $5,000 and returning to an appointment of $3,500 at will of the University Regents. But my reputation was undeserved. I had approached my friend, Charles R. Crane, who had been a backer of both Wilson and La Follette, and was afterwards ambassador to China. Crane gave me $2,500 per year, $1,000 for myself and $1,500 for a secretary and miscellaneous. My secretary had previously been paid from the funds for the Labor History. Crane's donation continued yearly until the Regents, after the War, raised my salary to $6,000, along with a similar general increase of salaries to meet the post-war inflation, and inserted in the budget a "secretary to Professor Commons," as well as provision for a half-time "assistant" graduate student. My successor on the Commission, Fred A. Wilcox, served three terms, eighteen years, with eminent distinction, until he was dropped by politics.

Crane was a notable traveler and sympathizer with oppressed races of Europe and Asia. He lived with them. He was a sociological discoverer. He opened my eyes to a new view of the Turk. He knew the Arabs. He knew Bokhara and Samarkand. He had long been a supporter of Professor Mazaryk, afterwards President of the Republic of Czecho-Slovakia. In his own private car, when relieved of his ambassadorship to China, he managed to return to America through Siberia and Russia at the peak of the Russian revolution, visiting the common people and avoiding the Soviet officials. He dictated this story to a stenographer and I wrote it out for a magazine article by him. He often came to Madison, where his daughter had married Dr. H. C. Bradley, eminent professor in our Medical Department. He always had something new and interesting. I dedicated to him my *Legal Foundations of Capitalism*. Surely I have been in luck with millionaires and socialists.

At the end of my term on the Industrial Commission, in June, 1913, I received a telegram from Senator La Follette, forwarded to me at Manhattan, Kansas, where I was delivering what I considered a failure as a Commencement address at the State Agricultural College. The tele-

gram stated that President Wilson, through Senator La
Follette, offered me the position of chairman of the new
Industrial Relations Commission. I had to answer immediately that I could not accept. I could not afford to ask
for another leave of absence from the University, this time
for the three years of the new Commission's life, after
having just returned to the University from two years on
the Wisconsin Industrial Commission. The Federal Commission had been created by Congress mainly on account
of the labor unrest, a part of which was the strike of the
structural iron-workers and the confessions of two of
their leaders in the shocking dynamite explosion which
destroyed the building of the *Los Angeles Times* and the
lives of twenty workers in the building.

On my return from Manhattan, Kansas, I stopped over
between trains at Kansas City and called on two of my
friends on the editorial staff of the *Kansas City Star*. They
told me of the rumor that Mr. Frank P. Walsh, the eminent criminal and labor lawyer of Kansas City, was being
considered for the position of chairman of the Industrial
Relations Commission, and asked me to go with them to
visit him at his office. On the way I told them of the
curious coincidence that I had just been offered the chairmanship but had been compelled to decline. We had been
in Walsh's office only a few minutes when a telegram was
delivered to him from President Wilson offering him the
chairmanship. He joined with my editorial friends in
urging me to accept a membership on the Commission.
I explained that I could not leave the University. It was
finally agreed that I might put in my vacation periods with
the Commission and organize an investigational staff

other than the staff employed for the public hearings. So I wired from Walsh's office to Senator La Follette that I would accept membership on the Commission, and Walsh wired at the same time to the President accepting the position of chairman. President Wilson appointed me as one of the three representatives of "the public" on the Commission, the others being Mr. Walsh and Mrs. J. Borden Harriman. Mrs. Harriman afterwards wrote an account of the Commission in her autobiographical sketch, *Pinafores and Politics.*

On the Industrial Relations Commission I eventually found myself in the hateful predicament of separating myself from my three labor colleagues. I finally drafted an independent report, signed by Mrs. Harriman and myself, and approved, with reservations on secondary boycott and representation of the public in labor disputes, by the three employer representatives. The other report was signed by Mr. Walsh and the three labor representatives. Individuals put in their own statements and dissents on each of the reports.

This division of five to four in the final report of the Commission came about on what appeared to me to be the issue as to whether the labor movement should be directed toward politics or toward collective bargaining. I thought, at that time, that the three labor representatives were being misled by the general labor unrest into throwing their movement into politics. I wanted them to avoid politics and to direct their energies toward what I knew was the policy of Samuel Gompers in building up strong organizations of self-governing unions able to meet the employers' organizations on an equality, and freed from the interference of politicians and what afterwards came to be known as "intellectuals" or "intelligentsia." Mr. Walsh seemed to me to typify the politician.

In our conferences and private conversations I discovered this issue forcing itself into the main issue before the Commission. The Railway Brotherhoods, not members of the American Federation of Labor, were represented on the Commission by the head of the conductors' organization, Mr. A. B. Garretson. They were then, I thought, being carried away by what afterwards came to be known as the "Plumb Plan" of representation of "labor" on the boards of directors of the railway corporations, as well as by the illusion of investment of their funds and the operation of such outside activities as banks, coal mines, office buildings, or even land speculation. I considered these schemes destructive of unionism, because they dissipated the strike funds and took labor over to the side of capitalists with a minority vote, leading them, by way of politics, into socialism or communism. At any rate I knew that labor unions had always been unsuccessful when they ventured into business or politics. I had met, in conferences, the then heads of the several railway brotherhoods, and knew that Garretson correctly represented them at that time. In my final report, read to the Commission, I earned the everlasting hatred of Garretson. Never afterwards would he speak to me, but gave me the royal snub, except when I cross-examined him, after the War, in a conference called by the United States Chamber of Commerce on the subject of transportation, shortly before the railways were turned back by the government to their private owners. In that conference Garretson advocated the Plumb Plan. It turned out eventually that I was correct in my fears. The Railway Engineers became practically bankrupt, and the reactions in the various brotherhoods led to election of officers committed against these outside ventures and against participation in capitalistic boards of directors, but in favor of turning their organizations back to "pure and simple unionism."

I got another curious angle on the railway brotherhoods. Mr. R. H. Aishton, president of the Chicago and Northwestern Railway Company, was a member of the Commission during the last six months of its existence. He was appointed in March, 1915, to fill the vacancy created by Mr. F. A. Delano who had resigned to accept membership on the Federal Reserve Board. I wished to have the support of Mr. Aishton, as a new member of the Commission, in the collective bargaining program which I was formulating. He had been engaged in many collective bargains with the railway brotherhoods. I appealed to him on the ground of conservatism. The political program of Walsh and Garretson, I argued, would not only get business into politics but it pointed toward communism and socialism. But the recognition of unions through collective bargaining would protect business and the nation against politics, radicalism, and communism, by placing a conservative labor movement in the strategic position. "My God," said Aishton, "you don't call them conservative, do you?"

So I learned that there were several meanings of the words "conservative," "radical," and "socialistic." To my academic mind "conservative" meant literally the dictionary meaning of "conservation" applied to existing institutions of property and liberty. To the practical business man in the midst of the conflict, "socialism" meant any movement or opinion, even trade-unionism, bent on reducing his profits or reducing his control over his own business.

I had much trouble in Wisconsin, both before and after my Industrial Relations experience, in distinguishing these meanings of words. I was charged with being an anarchist, or socialist, or communist, or, by a leading employer, with being the "most dangerous man in Wisconsin." Again I was charged with being a reactionary, lining up with big capitalists. Yet what I was always trying to do, in my academic way, was to save Wisconsin and the nation from politics, socialism, or anarchism, in dealing with the momentous conflict of "capital and labor." My distinctions in the meanings of words were too subtle, and my only refuge was silence, except in my classroom. I was not fitted for the rough-and-tumble of practical men, but I could admire them and could try, with my students, to analyze and classify their transactions.

The two representatives of the American Federation unions, Mr. J. B. Lennon, formerly president of the Journeyman Tailors' national union, and Mr. James O'Connell, formerly president of the Machinists' international union, had been displaced in their organizations largely by the socialistic element. But they held positions on the Executive Council of the American Federation of Labor. I thought they might see this big issue that was developing. So, without arguing the matter with them, or even consulting Mr. Gompers about it, I arranged a conference for them and myself with Mr. Gompers at his office. I took no part in the conference, hoping that they would work out, between themselves, the traditional stand, for forty years, of the American Federation of Labor. But there was no clash between Gompers and them, which I scarcely expected would occur between fellow members of the Executive Council in the presence of an outsider. Lennon and O'Connell joined with Garretson and Walsh in the final report. I was, indeed, preparing for what I felt must be my dissent from them, and I wanted Gompers at least to see, without my saying a word to him about it, that, if it came to an issue, I was standing for his own ideals of American unionism. After I made my report to the Commission, there were no harsh feelings on the part of Lennon or O'Connell toward me, and they remained my friends, like Gompers himself, as they had been since my Civic Federation days. In a magazine article on Gompers, after his death, I even declared myself a follower of Gompers. But Garretson was too enthusiastic and was carried off his feet by his sympathies. I admired him greatly for his long record and tireless energy in building up the conductors' organization. He remained in an advisory capacity to his union after his health had broken down, in 1919, until his death in 1931.

In harmony with our understanding at Kansas City, Mr. Walsh and I divided the supervision of the work of the Commission. He had charge of the public hearings, amounting eventually to eleven volumes, with his own staff. I had charge of the staff of investigators appointed on my recommendation. Mr. Walsh had selected a legal examiner for the hearings, who seemed to me to be too mild and inconsequential. I urged Walsh to take into his own hands the examination of witnesses, which he did. The other commissioners took part, if they saw fit. I considered these public hearings of much importance, although the witnesses merely stated their opinions and interpretations, and could not be budged into making any concessions that might be used toward reconciling their conflicting interests, or in making recommendations to Congress. My experience in the drafting of an immigration law under the Industrial Commission of 1901, my work with Easley in the National Civic Federation and with my colleagues of the Wisconsin Industrial Commission had given me a conviction that my own place was in private conference between the leaders of organizations in reaching agreements by conciliation. If such agreements could be reached then they could be embodied in detailed recommendations to Congress on future legislation and administration of labor laws.

Mr. Walsh and the labor representatives were of a different opinion regarding the purpose of the Commission. They wished to expose to the whole country the oppressions and injustices practiced by capitalists toward laborers, and to carry out the instructions of Congress in our enabling act of 1912, to "seek to discover the underlying causes of dissatisfaction in the industrial situation and report its conclusions thereon." Mr. Walsh succeeded brilliantly in this enlightenment of the public. His newspaper men, who went ahead of the Commission and arranged for the hearings, selected the outstanding leaders of capital, labor, and the general public. Their testimony, under Walsh's examination, attracted widespread interest through the press. The final report, made by Basil M.

Manly, whom Walsh selected for the purpose, was approved, with some exceptions by him and the labor representatives, and attracted wide publicity.

I knew quite well, through my work with Easley, La Follette, and the Wisconsin Commission that it would be impossible to bring employers and laborers to a state of "reasonableness" were it not for the concerted movements of politics, labor, agriculture, and capitalists which set up for each of them alternatives between which they must choose. It was this "choice of alternatives" instead of the pains and pleasures, or costs of production, of the economists, that I made my starting point for a realistic theory of political economy. It was realistic because it was the way in which practical men actually behaved. Mr. Aishton and the employers finally accepted and signed my report, with a few reservations. Mr. Walsh and the labor representatives strongly opposed it because they thought I proposed to set up a huge governmental administration that would deprive labor of its liberty.

What I proposed, in my report, supported by the employers and Mrs. Harriman, was a collective bargaining national labor board. It would be similar to what I had worked out for the Wisconsin Industrial Commission. Recently I received a letter from Mr. Bird, who had assisted me on the Wisconsin Commission and the Federal Industrial Relations Commission, saying that if Congress had followed my recommendations of 1915, there would have been no need in the War crisis of 1917 for an emergency war labor board nor in the peace crisis of 1933 for another national emergency labor board, for both of which he had been called in as investigator and negotiator.

He reminded me of a conversation I had with him in Washington at the beginning of the War, when he was connected with the emergency board and was himself "worked up" by the "obvious mistakes" of governmental officials. I made to him, he says, the philosophical observation, "Don't get discouraged. Haven't you learned yet that if human beings are given twelve ways to tackle a problem and eleven of them are wrong, they will try the eleven wrong ones first before they are forced to the twelfth and correct approach?" Well, I have been that way too. It is what I mean by my mistakes and experience.

Evidently I could not get across to my labor colleagues on the Industrial Relations Commission my ideas that collective bargaining, with the government acting only as a conciliator, should be made the basis of labor legislation and the administration of labor laws. Afterwards, in 1932, in Wisconsin, I was able to state the case more clearly to the leaders of the labor organizations when it came to enacting an unemployment insurance law. Here they had twenty years of experience with the collective bargaining arrangements of the State Industrial Commission, and thirty-five years' experience with their own separation of the labor movement itself into two organizations, a political party, the Social Democratic Party, and a labor organization, the Wisconsin Federation of Labor. They were giving their support to a bill which placed autocratic powers in the hands of a state commission. But they could understand, without any argument, when I pointed out to them that they had two conflicting "psychologies." They had a socialist psychology of political action and a trade-union psychology of collective bargaining. Which would they prefer in this new kind of labor legislation and administration? In politics they were a minority party, but in collective bargaining they were on an equality with the employers. They immediately changed their support to the collective bargaining bill. Its administrative provisions were quite similar to what I had proposed in my report as recommendations to Congress by the Industrial Relations Commission.

Eighteen years after that Commission's report the labor organizations of the nation find themselves suddenly compelled, but without experience in the field of collective bargaining under governmental administration, to participate in the formulation of "codes," the "working rules" of the National Industrial Recovery Administration. As a "pragmatic" theorist—a theorist who places experience foremost in the theories of political economy—I ultimately, at seventy-one years of age, have tried to bring together in my theory of "institutional economics" that which I was unsuccessful in putting across in practice to the labor representatives on the Commission in 1915.

I had, at that time, tried my best to do it. I asked Mr. Gompers to name trade-union representatives and he named Hugh Frayne, the Federation organizer in New York. I asked Mr. Magnus Alexander, organizer and head of the National Industrial Conference Board, the notable huge federation of some eighteen national employers' associations, to name employer representatives. He named F. C. Schwedtman, a leading manufacturer, and Walter Drew, of the National Erectors' Association. The latter had been attending practically all the hearings of the

Industrial Relations Commission. I had known Frayne, Alexander, Schwedtman, and Drew for several years. I selected as my aides my former students, William M. Leiserson and Francis H. Bird, of the Commission's investigational staff. Leiserson had organized the employment activities of the Wisconsin Industrial Commission. Afterwards he became perhaps the leading arbitrator of labor disputes in the United States. Bird had been my capable assistant in drafting the Industrial Commission Law of Wisconsin.

We conferees met together at the McAlpin Hotel in New York while the Commission was holding its public hearings. We began with the least disputatious issue—vocational education and apprenticeship—intending to get agreements and to draft bills for Congress on these points and then to proceed to the apparently irreconcilable issues of collective bargaining, open and closed shop, and the like. We were making much headway in these conferences when suddenly Mr. Walsh, as chairman, refused to sign any further vouchers for the salaries of any of the staff whom I had selected.

In the conduct of the investigation proper, outside these joint conferences, Mr. Walsh had agreed to the appointment of my friend Charles McCarthy of the Wisconsin Legislative Library. But Walsh and McCarthy, two Killarney Irishmen, could never agree. McCarthy was dropped by Walsh, and all of the investigators of my selection were dropped, or else resigned. I took the matter to the Commission, and proposed that all vouchers hereafter should be signed by a committee of three, Mr. Walsh as chairman and an employer member and a labor member of the Commission. The motion was defeated by a tie vote and Mr. Walsh was left in control of the funds. I, of course, had to retire to the University, and I only attended the final executive meeting of the Commission in Chicago, August, 1915. Yet I think I played the game on the level. I voted, by long-distance telephone, for Manly, Mr. Walsh's selection, as McCarthy's successor in charge of investigations.

The important thing for me now was what should be done with the unfinished investigations. Some of the investigators had already made a national reputation, especially Professor George E. Barnett of Johns Hopkins University, and Professor D. A. McCabe of Princeton University, who published afterwards their joint work on mediation and conciliation. Others would in future make a reputation, such as Leo Wolman, Sumner Slichter, William M. Leiserson, Francis H. Bird, Edwin E. Witte, Selig Perlman, Carl Hookstadt, and H. E. Hoagland.

What happened was that the Industrial Relations Commission had furnished salaries and clerical assistance for several months and even for more than two years, for capable investigators in their own special lines of interest. Mr. Manly acknowledged his indebtedness to them, except where he made modifications on his personal responsibility. He recommended that the Congress should be requested to print their reports as supplements to the report of the Commission. But Congress did not respond.

My worst anxiety was on account of Professor Robert F. Hoxie, of Chicago University. Indeed, Hoxie's fate, on being dropped by Walsh in the midst of his investigation of Scientific Management was a tragedy that burned into my life as a mere academic investigator. The issue between scientific management and organized labor was at that time, the most "irrepressible conflict" before the Commission. It involved the whole "open shop" and "closed shop" controversy. It even reached congressional action prohibiting the use of time and motion studies in government arsenals and other factories operated by the federal government. The Commission held public hearings on the subject, the most eminent of the proponents of scientific management appearing with explanations of their systems, and the trade-union representatives appearing in opposition. The Commission decided to make a special investigation of its own upon the subject. In order to prepare for the investigation the Commission held an executive and confidential hearing, with one witness, Mr. John P. Frey, editor of the *International Molders' Journal*, and I was permitted to be the only cross-examiner of Mr. Frey. He and I were close friends, having worked together at his office in Cincinnati for two weeks, in 1907, preparing a history of *Conciliation in the Stove Industry* for the United States Department of Labor. This executive hearing was designed to reduce the issue to all of the sub-headings to be investigated. Mr. Frey was undoubtedly the most scholarly and rational of all the labor leaders who were opposed to scientific management as then practiced. It was decided by the Commission to select a committee of three to make a field investigation of the subject. In this shop study the Commission selected Professor Hoxie as the investigator, to be assisted by Mr. Robert G. Valentine, representing employment management, and Mr. Frey, representing labor. They visited together a number of establishments and presented to the Commission a "final report" on which they had agreed. But the report was not printed by the Commission.

Mr. Hoxie had submitted to me, after he started on his investigation, an outline analysis and questionnaire of the whole subject, indicating the points to be investigated. I never before nor since have seen as comprehensive and detailed an outline of an investigation as this, on any economic subject. As printed it covered one hundred and sixty-five pages of his book, with only one hundred and thirty-seven pages devoted to the text. After his dismissal from the Commission he came to me at Madison, with all of his manuscripts, his notes, and his outline. He was in a nervous and incoherent state of mind. I was immediately alarmed. I went over all his material with him, explaining that he had the first really scientific study of scientific management, and it would be a serious misfortune if he did not publish as much of it as was already prepared. I promised to get a publisher for him, but he was worried about the share of the costs imposed upon him. Practically all of his notes on unfinished parts of his outline we eliminated. He went home seemingly cheerful, and put together what was already prepared, although he was anxious because he dreaded criticism in that he had not finished a complete piece of scientific work according to his ideals of workmanship. I think I made a mistake, which ended in his suicide.

I had spoken to the head of the firm of D. Appleton & Company about what I thought were the high-grade pieces of work left unfinished by the staff of the Industrial Relations Commission, suggesting to him that he should look up the investigators and arrange with them for completed books on their subjects. They published Hoxie on *Scientific Management* and on *Trade Unionism*.

Hoxie's brave wife, after his death, determined to publish his writings on trade unionism. I knew of his penetrating articles in the economic journals, which I thought could be reprinted, and thought also he must have unpublished manuscripts. She sent to me from Chicago a large package of reprints and manuscripts. I discarded the evidently unfinished materials and selected for her what I thought would make a telling book on Trade Unionism. She associated with herself Mr. Nathan Fine, and, after working up the materials, they submitted their work to several people for correction and revision. The book was brought out by Appleton in 1917, and a second edition in 1923. It has been generally recognized, in college teaching courses and elsewhere, as the first really outstanding analysis of American unionism, as well as a notable book on methods of investigation.

Hoxie's sudden death at the age of forty-eight, deprived American economic scholarship and the teaching profession of their most notable pioneer in labor research at the very point when he was beginning to round out his career. Afterwards a distinguished contributor to the study of labor economics said of him in the *Encyclopædia of the Social Sciences*, "A very large part of his best and most influential work found only oral expression in what must have been nearly the most realistic of American classrooms. . . . Hoxie possessed the keenest and most rigorous mind that has ever worked upon the problems of American labor organization." He added a comment on Hoxie's

Photoart and State Historical Society Wisconsin

IN MY OFFICE, 1932

VIEW FROM MY WINDOW, LAKE MENDOTA AND DISTANT HILLS, 1934

"unremitting attempt to penetrate to the causes of fundamental differences in principles and prejudices."

Thus ended, with Hoxie's suicide, a series of tragic events in my academic life. I had been compelled to separate myself from my labor friends and from the aggressive and astute lawyer whom I admired in his espousal of labor's interests. I had participated in the confused beginnings of a world-wide conflict that would end in class war and a war of nations. I saw then but dimly, and without much experimentation to go by, that which eventually I saw vividly as the clash of politics, unionism, communism, fascism, capitalism. I saw the initial suppressions, and even death, of the academic economists, with their futile appeals for reason in the din of mass conflict over scarcity of the world's resources. One day, in 1914, when the Commission was holding a heated discussion in executive session in Chicago, where I was trying vainly to depose Walsh, we were suddenly called out on the streets by the newsboys' cry, "Germany invades Belgium."

At a later date I was made president of the National Consumers' League on account of my well-known stand in favor of trade-unionism. I accepted, because of my admiration of Florence Kelley, the head of that organization.

As I now sit at my window looking back over the ten years of 1906 to 1915 I wonder how I found enough hours to do the variety of things I did. I never could endure a real vacation in the woods or fishing for more than one week at a time, except when I went down under a total collapse. During these years the collapse did not occur. I had an idea that a change of work was my best vacation. I persistently kept at my studies of economic theory in the

early morning hours, by going early to bed. The rest of
the day was a change to active work, in conference, teaching, supervising the work of others. My teaching was
wholly unsystematic—talking over with my classes the
outside work I happened to be on at the time, but always
drawing comparisons with similar situations and expoun-
ding or testing, at the same time, the theories of economists applied to the subject in hand.

But the collapse came in 1916. I left Madison before
the examination period and spent fifteen weeks at Lake
Tenderfoot on the Wisconsin-Michigan state line. I took
with me the books of several German economists and
studied them, making notes and revising my theories, for
two or three hours each morning in a cottage by myself.
The rest of the day I paddled my canoe, fished, walked
through the woods, got lost, ate meals at the summer
resort. During three or four weeks my wife and daughter
joined me. My son was working on a farm. I left Tenderfoot when the last boat left and snow had begun to fall.
Went to Mt. Vernon adjoining New York, to live with my
younger sister until February. There I walked or rode in
auto over the wonderful Westchester county as I had done
on bicycle with my boy fifteen years before when living
at the same Mt. Vernon.

In February, 1917, I returned to Madison and my teaching. The war scare was on, and I certainly was scared. I
lay awake at night horrified by the fate of the British boys
in the trenches. I saw, as though I were with them, the
British forces driven back to the sea and the submarines
driving the British food supply from the oceans. I was

terrified by what would happen if the British and French navies were taken over by the Germans merely by starving the island of Britain. The Germans, thereupon, with the greatest navy in the world, would take over Canada, Australia and the islands surrounding our Panama Canal. Then we should be compelled to fight Germany alone. I had hated Theodore Roosevelt's outburst for declaration of war at the invasion of Belgium. I admired Wilson for holding out for neutrality. But when Germany, in February, laid out a narrow path across the ocean for American vessels I saw the final starvation of England and our own inevitable war single-handed with Germany. My German students, afterwards, on the Rockefeller fellowships, said I need not have worried. Germany herself was starving. Well, she was conquering in 1917.

After war was declared, April 6, I could not yet openly express myself until I found whether my own boy would enlist. I said nothing to him about it, one way or another. The University boys, I knew, were intensely discussing the matter among themselves. Finally Jack enlisted, and a couple hundred of them started training on the University campus. I immediately went to the capitol to join with citizens and officials in organizing a system of state employment offices. While in conference one day on this subject I ran down to the street to see my boy, with some two hundred other students, marching in their students' caps and clothes four abreast to the train that would take them to the officers' training camp at Ft. Sheridan. Then I returned to the conference on employment offices. My son became second lieutenant; about forty of the Wisconsin boys landed, in September, 1918, at Archangel, where their fighting continued against the Bolsheviki, shut in by the Arctic ice, until six months after the armistice. He did not come home until August, 1919. My boy disappeared suddenly from Madison August 1, 1930. The doctors whom I consulted traced his mental aberration, with its mania of persecution by concealed shots, anonymous letters, and other imagined attacks, back to the forests of arctic Russia where he and fifteen privates retreated for nine days without sleep, surrounded by Bolsheviki. His record was "splendid" according to our state adjutant-general. From the date of his disappearance in 1930 began my last total collapse, from which, by the help of my Friday Niters and my dear Doctor "Joe" Evans, head of the Wisconsin State Hospital attached to the University, I am now slowly recovering.

Our conferences on state employment offices soon developed a plan, to be coördinated with the Federal offices, and I was placed in charge under the State Industrial Commission. We estimated the cost to the State treasury at $10,000, but when it came to Governor Emanuel Philipp he refused the appropriation. I necessarily then dropped out, along with my students who were assisting me. During the six years of Governor Philipp's incumbency I was not called in for conferences of any kind, and gave my whole time to my classroom. So it has been under stalwart and Democratic governors, though I was always more conservative than I wanted to be. Only Progressives wanted me and I was often too conservative for them. I made a speech to a mass meeting of University students in favor of enlistment for the War. A few were pacifists and did not enlist, even going to Leavenworth for conscience' sake. I did not play up President Wilson's "Make the world safe for democracy." That seemed buncombe to me. I played up the inevitableness of a war single-handed with Germany if England and France were defeated. "Make the world safe for America. Do it now before it is too late." That was my war scare.

On my trip to Washington to confer with the federal employment administration about fitting the State system into the Federal system, I called on Senator La Follette at his office in the Capitol. I found him with Senator Stone of Missouri. They had been the two outstanding "willful senators" in opposition to Wilson's message for declaration of war. We had a heated discussion. La Follette said, "I am determined to get us out of this war as soon as I honorably can. My advices from Wisconsin show that the people of the State are five to one in favor of my stand." This alarmed me. On our walk from his office toward the Union Station, neither of us could say a word. I saw then his unconquerable will with his jaw shut tight. Never before had I come against it in my own person. I determined that, when I should get back to Wisconsin, I would do what I could to elect opponents of La Follette. I had conferences with his opponents. I attended a congressional nominating convention; spoke in favor of Nils P. Haugen, La Follette's first candidate for governor in 1894 and holding, at that time, a position on the Tax Commission to which La Follette had appointed him. But I was too naïve. The reactionary Republicans had control. I voted to make the nomination of their candidate unanimous. He had his speech already written. He knew what was coming. He was elected to Congress. I took my medicine. I was now a reactionary.

What a tragedy for me! For fifteen years I had been an intimate in La Follette's household. In 1912 I worked at his home in Washington for two weeks, while he attended to his duties in the Senate, in preparing his presidential campaign platform to be released to the press at the time of his coming address, in Philadelphia, at a national meeting of the leading newspaper and magazine writers. I had become acquainted with several of them at his home. Woodrow Wilson was also to address that meeting. La Follette's platform occupied several columns in such newspapers as published it. On the evening, at five o'clock, when he was leaving his home for the dinner meeting at Philadelphia, my last word to him was, what I had been insisting all along, that he should speak not longer than thirty minutes. The people of the East, at a dinner like that, would not stand for three-hour speeches with which he held audiences in Wisconsin, nor for the long and detailed platform on which I was helping him. He was, up to that time, the undoubted leader of the Progressives in the nation. He had made a wonderful campaign, including large out-door meetings in the West during the bitter cold of the preceding December. He promised me he would not speak more than thirty minutes. But he spoke more than two hours, I was told. His newspaper and magazine friends, as I met them afterwards, were bewildered and chagrined. They listened to the charges that he was drunk. I did not believe them. In all of my acquaintance with him he and I smoked the blackest of cigars, but he never drank, except occasionally when we were finishing our work and were getting ready for bed.

One of his anxieties was whether Theodore Roosevelt would support him. I made an appointment with Roosevelt at the Aldine Club, New York. I put it to Roosevelt, Would he support La Follette? He answered in the Rooseveltian way, "Yes; tell him to go ahead." At the Philadelphia meeting were many Roosevelt supporters, all of them, as far as I knew, supporting La Follette. The next day, with almost one accord, they declared for Roosevelt.

I left Washington the same night when La Follette left for Philadelphia. I did not see him when he returned. I never had the effrontery to speak to him of the Philadelphia meeting. I could not possibly say, Why did you speak more than thirty minutes? I buried my grief. My idol had fallen. I was told afterwards by intimates of his family how, for several days, he was in the depths of mental depression. He thought his friends had deserted him. And now, after twenty years, to think that I would desert him within five years on the question of war! I had helped him on his bill for the valuation of railways, and testified before the Senate Committee. He knew that I had not deserted him, but nothing was said of the Philadelphia meeting. After the War, in 1924, I attended the meeting at Cleveland which nominated him as an independent candidate for President. I wrote articles for his candidacy in the magazines. He carried only his own state. It was grief to me that, during the years following 1917, when I was often in Washington, I could not get up courage to visit him at his home. I was afraid of his family. I received no invitation. I met him and his son Robert on public affairs at his office in the Senate building. They were to me the same as ever. I supported eagerly the younger Robert for Senator and Phil for Governor. Phil called me in continuously on measures that he was promoting, and in conferences with railway presidents and leading manufacturers. I enlisted my students. One of them, William E. Chalmers, from Brown University, was paid a salary by W. T. Rawleigh, campaign manager for La Follette in 1924, as my liaison officer with Phil and the different branches of government and University needed to assemble statistics and draft bills.

I had known Mr. Rawleigh since 1907. He had started as a Wisconsin boy making up recipes for farmers' livestock and delivering the preparations personally in his one-horse wagon. He now had 6,000 automobiles, visiting nearly every farmer's home in the United States twice a year. He had purchasing stations throughout the world, and a dozen distributing stations in the United States. I had helped him on municipal monopolies when he was mayor of Freeport, Illinois, where his huge factory was located. He was enraged over the Smoot-Hawley tariff. He asked me to head up an investigation of the tariff. I agreed to do so without compensation if he would furnish me an assistant, Chalmers, and additional compensation for my secretary. Three of my colleagues took leave of absence from the University, their equivalent salaries paid by Rawleigh. Graduate students were put on his payroll. Only one instruction he gave us: "Find the facts." Though an ardent free trader he knew that I was a protectionist. We organized a large class on the tariff. Some eight or ten monographs were published and others are now going through the press. Certain students who took part are now professors in agricultural colleges. Their monographs were their dissertations for the Ph.D. degree. So again, by a millionaire's help, I financed University research and instruction, along with assistance to the second generation of my beloved and tragic La Follette of the first generation.

I had learned, in my Indiana and Syracuse days, to look upon the money question as the most important of all labor problems. I visited, one early morning in 1894, the camp of "Kelly's Army" from Southern California, which had tramped across the deserts to join Coxey's army on the march to Washington. I talked with a jeweller. He had left his unemployed relatives at Los Angeles because he was the only one physically able to stand the hunger march. I talked with others. To my mind they were as fine a set of workingmen as I had ever known. They told me of their harsh treatment by the railway companies and policemen on that long march. I attended the Populist meetings in Indiana. I saw the common misfortune of farmers and laborers.

Again, at the height of inflation in the summer of 1919, I was financed by leading paper manufacturers of Wisconsin to visit, with several of my students, the best factories we could find with the best labor management. We visited about thirty, together and separately. We published our findings in a book which we named *Industrial Government*. What my paper manufacturers said they earned for their money, when I reported to them, was that the best way to beat the unions was "to beat them to it." This conclusion startled me. I had not expected it.

At our hotels in New York we brought together at

dinner time the business agent of the employers and the business agent of the union in the clothing industry. They agreed on the facts. The union had a wage-scale of $50 per week for pressers and had imposed a fine on any member accepting more than the union scale. They had their union committees to hunt down violators. The employers had their pickets on the lookout for the union committees, in order to hide violators of the union maximum. The employers were paying as high as $125 per week for pressers.

In another industry the employer claimed that wages had been advanced threefold and labor output had been reduced two-thirds, but they were making a profit by the rise in prices of their product. Many similar examples were found. Two years later, in 1921, those same employees, with millions besides, were on the streets begging for work. The employers were "liquidating" them, by slashing wages and speeding up. In my testimony before a Congressional Committee, in 1927, on "price stabilization," I joined the labor problem with the money problem. The business cycle first demoralizes labor, then pauperizes labor, then coerces labor. The most important labor problem was the stabilization of the average of employers' wholesale prices.

I never had an opportunity to study the money problem in the banks as I had studied the labor problem in the factories. I had read Fisher's and Wicksell's theories and plans. The National Monetary Association as a successor to Fisher's Stable Money League, was organized in 1922. I was made president. The organization was financed by Mr. W. Catchings, whom I had known during the War, a successful "Wall Street" financier. My expenses, but no compensation, were to be paid. My first job was to convert Henry Ford and Thomas Edison from their paper money theories to our stabilization theories. I visited Ford and Edison with my blue prints of prices. When Ford declared for Coolidge, in the campaign of 1924, my usefulness was at an end. Mr. Catchings told me that he was sorry but he had to choose between going along with his people and supporting the Association. The Association was reorganized by Norman Lombard under the name of the Stable Money Association with another president. In the session of Congress, 1928, Lombard raised $2,500 for my expenses in Washington to assist Congressman Strong of Kansas in promoting, before the House Committee, his bill for the stabilization of prices by the Federal Reserve System. I had the regular half-year's leave of absence, with pay from the University, which I had earned by teaching without pay in summer sessions. My wife and I had planned a trip to Europe, but she died, after an operation, on January 1, 1928. I wanted to work at something as hard as possible. Lombard's donor of $2,500, whose name I do not know to this day, enabled me to take to Washington my daughter Rachel as my secretary, and the University permitted me to take also my statistical assistant, Myrtle Starr, on the University pay roll. She compiled for me several charts used in the hearings. I spent five months with Congressman Strong, and ended with a breakdown of four weeks in my hotel. My hotel doctor encouraged me by saying "We will bring you through to eighty-five years of age." I wrote, in my bed, a "statement," instead of giving a concluding testimony before the House Committee, and the statement was printed in the report of the Committee. I afterwards wrote on stabilization of prices for magazines and rounded out a theory of "Banker Capitalism" for my *Institutional Economics,* as the economic successor to the stages of Merchant Capitalism and Employer Capitalism. My theorizing ended with March, 1933, but I set my students at work on a comparison of the "automatic recovery" from the depression after 1897, during which I had compiled my first index number of prices, with the new Roosevelt and his "managed recovery" after 1933, aimed toward his managed restoration and stabilization of prices and industry.

Thus, in my concluding ten or twelve years, I was plunged into the midst of another conflict of interests. This time it was not the wage conflicts of "capital and labor," but the price conflicts within capitalism itself. "Labor" was helpless, bewildered, demoralized, pauperized, coerced by this world conflict over prices. I could not blame the capitalists. They, too, were victims. I saw banker capitalism at work from the inside. I spent much time with the Federal Reserve bank in New York and the Federal Reserve Board at Washington. I learned from Governor Benjamin Strong of the New York bank how he operated with the bank rate and the open market operations to "mop up" credit or to expand credit on the money market, and how they had to regulate credit in order to enable England to return to the gold standard. Curiously enough, though I was a late comer in the field of banking, I was, in December, 1924, the first to expound to economists at the American Economic Association the principles of control of the money market by a central bank through buying and selling securities on the open market at current prices. This was something new to me. I had not seen it in the books on money and credit. One of the economists, a specialist in banking, said to me, "I have seen it all along and am kicking myself now that I did not understand it." I understood it because Benjamin Strong and his assistants in the bank had explained it to me.

I attended one of the monthly luncheons of about thirty of the forecasters of big business and banks in February, 1923, assembled from different parts of the country and even from England. We guessed, around the table, how soon and how high the then amazing rise of wholesale prices would reach its peak. The average guess came at a rise from the index number of 138 at the end of 1921 to an index number of 172 a year ahead, in March, 1924. The average rise of prices had been going on at the rate of $1\frac{1}{2}$ per cent per month, more rapidly, a part of the time, than the rise in 1919. In the New York bank there was much alarm about this rise, culminating in a confidential letter from Washington about the inflationist tendencies of authorities there. I went to Washington the first week in February and visited my old newspaper friend, then secretary to President Harding. He introduced me to Mr. Crissinger, Comptroller of the Currency and member of the Federal Reserve Board. Crissinger said to me, "We know what to do but we do not know just when and how much." The what and the when were open market sales of securities, which they had already begun in 1922, and the raising of rediscount rates which they had not yet begun. The rates, however, were raised two or three weeks after my interview. The rise of prices stopped in April, 1923, at 156 and fell to about 145 in 1924, instead of going on to our forecasters' peak of 172 in March, 1924.

No wonder that I immediately made "Timeliness," in a speech before our Monetary Association, the most important factor in the concerted action of bankers and business men, and defined timeliness as doing the right thing at the right time and with the right degree of power. Later I tied up this timeliness with the strategic transactions and forecasting that determine the future transactions, while routine transactions go on in the hands of subordinates. This academic conclusion, I admit, is not of much help to business men and politicians, because they are in the midst of action, and must act *now,* while the economist may wait and criticize long afterwards. But it enables me to understand the opportunism and strategy of great leaders, like Carnegie, Rockefeller, or President Roosevelt, who can act only on one thing at a time in the midst of the many conflicting things that must wait until the then strategic one is controlled. I call it a volitional theory of multiple causation, expanded from the economists' theory of "limiting and complementary factors."

I learned how difficult strategic transactions were and yet how crucial. When the post-war inflation was sending prices upward, in early 1919, two members of the Federal Reserve Board considered whether they should not resign rather than consent to the low rates of discount and easy money policy of the Board. A grave mistake was made during 1919 which had to be corrected too late, in June, 1920, by raising the bank rate to seven per cent. The depression of 1921, instead of being a "conspiracy" in June,

1920, to depress prices was a compelled result of lack of
timeliness in raising the rate fifteen months before, in
1919. The Board learned, in the inflation of 1922 and
1923, what only two members knew in the inflation of
1919. Yet the latter had failed, at that time, to call the
attention of the nation to it by failing to resign. I saw in
1919 demoralization of labor and in 1921 its pauperization,
because the Federal Reserve System, in reality a central
bank of the world in 1919 because it had control of the
world's gold, failed to do the right thing at the right time
and with the right degree of world-wide economic control which the system then had. When it came to later
times, after 1925, the system had lost its world-wide control because other nations had gold. Thus I drew my
theories from what I saw of the inside workings, the personalities and even my own little participation in the national politics of Banker Capitalism.

During intervals in this ten-year experience with banker
capitalism I piled up experience in two other fields. The
Association of Rolled Steel Consumers, in the West and
South, after the doubling of railway freight rates on account of the War, found that the practice of the steel
industry in making "delivered prices," including freight,
from the single basing point Pittsburgh, instead of f.o.b.
prices at their several factories, acted against their custom-
ers in the discriminatory high prices paid for their principal raw material. It was named, in the parlance of the
trade, the Pittsburgh-Plus practice. Eighteen state legislatures adopted resolutions against the practice. Four states,
Illinois, Wisconsin, Minnesota, and Iowa, made appropria-

tions with which their attorneys general should prosecute the leader of the steel industry, the United States Steel Corporation, before the Federal Trade Commission. The attorneys general asked me to visit Washington and ascertain the progress already made by the legal staff of the Federal Commission. There I met an eminent economist friend who advised me not to enlist in the case because the practice was the "natural law of supply and demand." Afterwards, in the hearings, the lawyer of the Steel Corporation argued that the practice was a "custom" of several generations and therefore sanctioned by time.

I reported back from Washington what I thought was the difference between the legal approach and the economic approach. The lawyers were basing their prosecution on the theory of monopoly; the economists would base theirs on a theory of discrimination. The attorneys general, after hearing me, proposed through my friend, Herman L. Ekern, Attorney General of Wisconsin, that I should take charge of this case with two leading economists of the country. We agreed on Frank A. Fetter and William Z. Ripley. I was to get leave of absence from the University for one semester, the fall of 1923, at double my University salary. I took with me my University assistant, Donald E. Montgomery. Fetter and Ripley were paid lump sums. Fetter, of Princeton, worked out, in a most logical way, the economic theory of a free and non-discriminatory market. Ripley, of Harvard, long an authority on railway regulation, brought to bear on this manufacturing industry his extensive knowledge of the practice of discrimination in the railway industry. I studied the court decisions and wrote out a brief for our lawyer

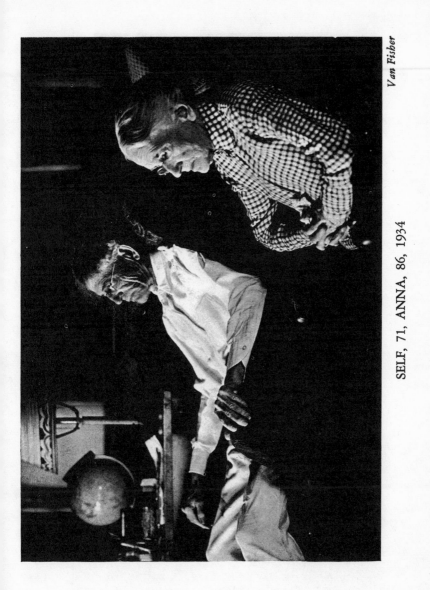

Van Fisber

SELF, 71, ANNA, 86, 1934

MY FRIDAY NITERS, 1930

on an economic interpretation of the history of the common law from what I called the early period of Scarcity to the Nineteenth Century period of Abundance, and now, in the Twentieth Century, the period of reasonable stabilization. Our lawyer could not make use of my brief because I could not assure him that it, as an "expert" opinion, conformed to the accepted opinions of economists. But I inserted it afterwards, almost verbatim, as a section in my book on institutional economics, comparing it with the economists' "materialistic interpretation of history" taken over from Karl Marx. I wrote in September, 1924, for the *American Economic Review,* an account of the "delivered price system" in the steel market. Fetter developed, from his Pittsburgh-Plus brief, his notable book on *The Masquerade of Monopoly* published in 1931. Our capable lawyer, Harold Pickering, from Superior, Wisconsin, had used Fetter's brief and diagrams before the Federal Commission in explaining the principles of a fair, equal and non-discriminatory market. He was immediately taken from Wisconsin by the opposing attorney for the Steel Corporation to become a member of a leading firm of lawyers in New York. Montgomery returned to Wisconsin to be the economist of the State Market Commission.

These conferences of mine, with Fetter, Ripley and Montgomery, as well as with our attorneys general and the lawyers of the Federal Trade Commission, rounded out remarkably my efforts to coördinate the theories of law and economics. We economists, supported by our attorneys general, wanted to enter into conferences with officials of the Steel Corporation in order to reach an agreement to be submitted to the Federal Trade Commission for amendment and approval. We wanted collective bargaining between the Association of Rolled Steel Consumers and the leaders of the steel producing interests. But the Commission notified us that we would not be permitted to testify as expert witnesses if we did such a thing. So we carried on the legal fight and clash of interests instead of collective bargaining and reconciliation of interests. We won in the legal fight. The Steel Corporation notified the Commission of their acceptance, reserving appeal to the courts if they should so wish. Ten years later, with the incoming of NIRA codes, our collective bargaining idea was extended on a grand scale by Presidential decree to the steel and other industries, but I am informed they are returning the steel industry to the discriminatory delivered-price system and Fetter's Masquerade of Monopoly.

While I was at work on the Pittsburgh-Plus case, in 1923, Leo Wolman called on me, representing the collective agreement of manufacturers and the union in the men's clothing industry of Chicago, on unemployment insurance. They asked me to become chairman at a salary of $7,000. I found that what they had agreed upon was exactly the plan which I had worked out for state legislation and had published in *The Survey* magazine in 1921. I went to Chicago for a week to get acquainted. Then in January, 1924, after the Pittsburgh-Plus work was completed, I spent the remaining month of my leave of absence in Chicago organizing the system. I had the aid of a notable body of men who had negotiated the agreement. Besides Wolman, economist for the Amalgamated Clothing Workers, there were Sidney Hillman, national president of the union; Earl Dean Howard, of Northwestern University and labor manager for Hart, Schaffner and Marx; officials of the leading clothing manufacturers; Bryce Stewart, manager of the employment office for the union; and Benjamin Squires, a former student of mine and now chairman of the arbitration board. When I left, after eighteen months, Squires was made also chairman of the Unemployment Insurance Board.

What I had to do was to organize seventy boards into one board, and to provide that I should leave Madison only once a month, at week-ends, to attend sessions of the boards. I was seventy chairmen. This was because the plan provided for "establishment funds" instead of a "market fund." The union had contended for a market fund wherein contributions of all establishments and all employees would be merged in a common fund and then paid out to all of the unemployed. The employers contended for separate establishment funds because they did not want to be made responsible for the unemployment in their competitors' establishments. The latter had been my original plan, based on my experience in administration of the accident-prevention and accident-insurance laws of Wisconsin. I found, in Chicago, that I had correctly sized up the competitive psychology and individual initiative of American business men. They did not want to be made responsible for the mistakes, misfortunes, or inefficiency of their competitors. So they insisted on separate establishment funds and separate boards of administration for each establishment. The union had finally agreed, and so I was made seventy chairmen.

A compromise, however, had to be made. There were

some two hundred small contractors, unable to set up establishment funds, and they were merged into one market fund of their own with one board of administration for the two hundred.

Then there were about sixty-five medium-sized establishments, which, although each had its separate fund, yet were willing to act together with one board. So, some three hundred separate establishments were reduced to two boards of administration. But the two largest establishments insisted each on its own board. So, once a month I had to attend four board meetings in different places. We fixed it up in advance, so that the boards met in sequence for about a half-hour each. This was possible because the union representation was the same on each board. Also because Bryce Stewart, formerly deputy commissioner in the Canadian Department of Labor and now employed by the Chicago union, divided his time between operating the employment office and installing and operacting what to me was a marvellous system of employment records for 25,000 employees and three hundred establishments. He became the leading authority in the country on unemployment insurance, leaving Chicago to conduct investigations with the "Industrial Counsellors" in New York, financed by John D. Rockefeller, Jr. My work, after the first month, was entirely routine. I had to decide only one disputed claim during the eighteen months. Needless to say, I brought all of the proceedings, the agreements, and all records to Madison, where I worked over them with my students in drafting and redrafting the original bill for legislation in Wisconsin.

My twenty-five years' experience, from the Pittsburgh

Survey of 1907 to the unemployment insurance law of 1932 in Wisconsin, with the development of my ideas on administration and collective bargaining I wrote up finally in 1933 for my *Institutional Economics*. At my seventieth anniversary, with an audience of some two hundred colleagues, students, citizens, and officials of the State, the most satisfying speech, to me, was that of the business agent of the Chicago Clothing Workers who said, "You are responsible for seven million dollars, one million a year, paid out as unemployment benefits to the members of my union."

So ended my seventy years. Now, with my sister, who is eighty-six, at my side, I am trying to recover from my latest collapse, that I may live out the eighty-five years promised me in Washington by my doctor at the Powhatan Hotel in 1928.

POSTSCRIPT.—My sister Anna was killed in an auto accident while this book was in press.

[PUBLISHER'S NOTE, 1963.—John R. Commons died on May 11, 1945, very nearly fulfilling his doctor's prediction.]

Survey of 1907 to the management lecture list of 1931 in Wisconsin, with the varied report of my ideas on administration and collective bargaining, I welcome finally in 1931 for my remanagement Document? As my seventieth anniversary, with an audience of some two hundred collegiate students, critics, and curious of the past, one more satisfying speech, coming was that of the business agent of the Chicago Clothing Workers who said, "You are responsible for seven million dollar, organizing a year, paid out as unemployment, beating to the members of my union."

To end your service here, I hope, when my strength is still on the early side, I am ready to receive from my later colleague that I may live out the declining years.
— printed me in *Washington Review* foreword at the Sixtieth head in 1938.

Postscript — Ms. Anne Anne was killed in an auto accident while the last was in press.

[Publisher's note: 1903—John RR Commons, died Mrs. B. 1955, very usual, building his monuments the deacon.]